**Rum & Reggae's Grenadines,
Including St.Vincent and Grenada**

Rum & Reggae's™

Grenadines

Including
St. Vincent & Grenada

FIRST EDITION

Jonathan Runge

Rum & Reggae Guidebooks, Inc.
Prides Crossing, Massachusetts • 2003

First Edition
Second Printing

ISBN: 978-1893675-094
LIBRARY OF CONGRESS CONTROL NUMBER: 2003094265

Book design by Valerie Brewster, Scribe Typography
Cover design by Jonathan Runge and Valerie Brewster
Cover photo by Tony Lulek
Back cover photo by Digital Vision
Author photo by Vincent-louis Apruzzese of behemothmedia.com
Illustrations by Eric Orner (Illustration on page 11 by David M.W. Greer)
Maps by Tony Lulek and Bruce Withey, and Jonathan Runge

Printed in the United States.

For Brendan and Judith

The Grenadines,
St. Vincent
& Grenada

KINGSTOWN ●   ST. VINCENT

```
0          10          20
├──────────┼──────────┤
        MILES
```

— BEQUIA

ATLANTIC OCEAN

CARIBBEAN SEA

  —MUSTIQUE

— CANOUAN

MAYREAU

—TOBAGO CAYS

UNION ISLAND —

—PALM ISLAND

PETIT ST. VINCENT

PETITE MARTINIQUE

CARRIACOU

GRENADA

ST. GEORGE'S ●

CONTENTS

The Larger Grenadines

Bequia 19

TOURISTO SCALE: 🐒🐒🐒🐒

The Smaller Grenadines

St. Vincent and Grenada

Lodging and Restaurant Key

Note: We have used a number of symbols and terms to indicate prices and ambiance. Here are the code breakers.

Lodging Symbols

C   telephone number

🖋   fax number

🖳   web site URL and/or e-mail address

$ room rates

🍴   meal plan

CC   major credit cards*

be sure to ask if your credit card is accepted when making reservations

★   This is a *Rum & Reggae* "best of category" establishment.

Lodging Rates

Prices are *rack rates* for double (two people) in high season—generally mid-December through mid-April—unless otherwise noted. Many hotels, especially the larger ones, offer specials (pay for five nights, stay for seven) that can lower the prices. Summer rates are as much as 50 percent cheaper. Unless otherwise noted, prices for singles are the same or slightly less.

Dirt Cheap	under $50
Cheap	$51–$100
Not So Cheap	$101–$150
Pricey	$151–$200
Very Pricey	$201–$300
Wicked Pricey	$301–$400
Ridiculous	$401–$500
Beyond Belief	$501–$600
Stratospheric	$601 and up!

Hotel tax in St. Vincent and its Grenadines is 7 percent; in Grenada, Carriacou, and Petite Martinique it's 8 percent. Expect a service charge of 10 percent added to your hotel bill; you are not expected to leave any additional tips. If in doubt, ask at the time of booking (and while you're at it, ask at the front desk how the service charge will be distributed to employees—at some hotels, not all of this charge actually makes it into their pocket).

Lodging and Meal Codes ⑪

All hotel prices are assigned a corresponding code that relates to the meals that are included in the rates. In the Grenadines, many hotels incorporate meals into the rates—take this factor into consideration if you are comparing rates between properties.

EP	**European Plan**—No meals included.
CP	**Continental Plan**—Continental breakfast (bread, cereal, juice, coffee) included.
BP	**Breakfast Plan**—Full hot breakfast included.
MAP	**Modified American Plan**—Full breakfast and dinner included.
FAP	**Full American Plan**—Full breakfast, lunch, and dinner included (sometimes with an afternoon "tea" or snack as well).
All-Inclusive	All meals, beer, wine, and well drinks (house brands) are included, most or all on-site activities, and usually tax and service charges.

Restaurant Prices

Prices represent per-person cost for the average meal from soup to nuts.

$	under $10	$$$$	$31–$40
$$	$11–$20	$$$$$	over $40
$$$	$21–$30		

PREFACE

Rum & Reggae's Grenadines, Including St. Vincent and Grenada is the eighth book to be published by Rum & Reggae Guidebooks, Inc. Writing these books is now a team effort. For *Rum & Reggae's Grenadines, Including St. Vincent and Grenada* — David Swanson was a contributor. Here is his bio.

David Swanson is a San Diego–based freelance writer who has been traveling to the Caribbean for more than 17 years. Although he enjoys all of the islands to varying degrees, he has particularly enjoyed discovering the region's more exotic corners, including Haiti, Cuba (in 1989, just as the Soviet Union was terminating aid), and the summit of Montserrat's smoldering volcano. Swanson's stories have appeared in assorted magazines and more than 45 North American newspapers, including *Caribbean Travel and Life, American Way, National Geographic Traveler, The Los Angeles Times, The Boston Globe, The Miami Herald, The Dallas Morning News, The Globe and Mail*, and others.

We hope you enjoy the book. Please be sure to visit our Web site at www.rumreggae.com and check out our quarterly newsletter.

ACKNOWLEDGMENTS

Contrary to what you might think, writing a book on the Grenadines is not very glamorous. We've always said that the most glittering part about this business is answering the "So what do you do?" question at cocktail parties. It's all uphill from there. We do not spend our days on the beach or by the pool sipping a rum punch. Well, okay, sometimes we do. But most of the time we were running around, coordinating ferry and plane schedules, checking out this or that and complaining about the heat. Just when we start to get comfortable in a place, it's time to uproot ourselves and start all over again. Try doing that at least every other day, and you'll begin to know what we mean.

Fortunately, some wonderful people helped us out along the way. We'd like to take this opportunity to sincerely thank those who did. First and foremost are the folks at the St. Vincent and the Grenadines and the Grenada tourist boards and their public relations representatives, including Celia Ross, Edwin Frank, Nicole Moultrie, Melissa Viola, Tammy Peters, and Kim Greiner. If we overlooked your name, sorry, but thanks for your help!

Rum & Reggae's Grenadines, Including St. Vincent and Grenada is published by Rum & Reggae Guidebooks, Inc. I have a lot of helpers and all deserve a hearty thanks. First and foremost, a lot of credit for this book goes to David Swanson, my chief Caribbean writer. My warmest gratitude also goes to the following: our fabulous new and wonderfully easygoing book designer, Valerie Brewster, of Scribe Typography; our very talented web designer, Michael Carlson; our corporate illustrator and Disney animation megastar, Eric Orner; our cartographers (besides myself), Bruce Withey, and Tony Lulek ; our cover photographer, Tony Lulek; our new distributor, Independent Publishers Group, its chief, Curt Matthews, and its great staff; our legal team at Sheehan, Phinney, Bass & Green of Maria Recalde, Kerry

Scarlott, and Doug Verge; our printer, Transcontinental Printing, and its terrific rep, Ed Catania; and our patient copy editor and indexer, Judith Antonelli.

There were several people who helped in other ways. Many thanks to Duncan Donahue and Tom Fortier, Nan Garland, Elvis Jiménez-Chávez and Chris Lawrence, and Tony Lulek.

Finally, a wicked thanks to my business partner, marketing and sales director, budding author and right-hand man, Joe Shapiro; and to my parents, Eunice and Albert Runge, for their continued enthusiasm and support.

Finally, a can of dolphin-safe tuna to my cat and guardian angel, Jada.

To all who helped, many thanks — YAH MON!

Jonathan Runge
Author and Publisher
Rum & Reggae Guidebooks, Inc.
Prides Crossing, Massachusetts
June 1, 2003

INTRODUCTION

Travel with an Opinion.™ That's how we describe our distinct point of view. *Rum & Reggae's Grenadines, Including St. Vincent and Grenada* is not your typical tourist guidebook to these fabled sailing waters. We like to say that the Rum & Reggae series is written for people who want more out of a vacation than the standard tourist fare. Our reader is more sophisticated and independent. He's also more active — be it scuba diving, windsurfing, art seeking, hiking, sailing, golfing, playing tennis, exploring, or cocktailing. Or she's more particular, in search of places that are secluded, cerebral, spiritual, or très branché (if you have to ask what the latter means, those places are not for you).

This book differs from other guidebooks in another way. Instead of telling you that everything is "nice" — nice, that is, for the average Joe — *Rum & Reggae's Grenadines, Including St. Vincent and Grenada* offers definitive opinions. We will tell you what's fantastic and what's not, from the point of view of someone who loathes the tourist label and the other bland travel books whose names we won't mention.

We'll take you throughout these islands and share our recommendations of where to go (and where not to go). More important, we filter out all the crap for you so you can have fun reading the book and enjoy your vacation and keep the decision making to a minimum. We wish we had had this book when we were doing our research. It would have made our job a helluva lot easier. We would have had more time to kick back and get sand between our toes.

So mix yourself a rum punch (we even provide the best recipe), put on some Bob Marley, and sit back and let *Rum & Reggae's Grenadines, Including St. Vincent and Grenada,* take you on your own private voyage to feel all right.

Rum & Reggae's Grenadines, Including St. Vincent and Grenada

Before You Go

Climate

The weather in the Grenadines is about as close to perfect as anywhere on Earth. The temperature rarely dips below 70°F/21°C or scales to above 90°F/32°C (at sea level). It gets slightly cooler at night in the mountains, but since there's little in the way of restaurants or accommodations you probably won't need anything beyond a light sweater, even in winter. The sun shines almost every day. Rainfall comes in the form of brief, intense cloudbursts, quickly followed by sunshine. It's pretty hard not to get a tan.

The reasons for this ideal climate are the constant temperature of the ocean—about 80°F year-round—and the steady trade winds from Africa. The Caribbean is not susceptible to the harsh weather patterns of the middle latitudes. The only weather peril to a Grenadines vacation is an occasional summer tropical depression or hurricane, which can make life very exciting. However, the islands described in this book lie on the edge of the hurricane belt, so major tempests are rare. In general, we don't advise against traveling to the Caribbean during the six-month June–November storm season—after all, we come here often during that period to enjoy smaller crowds and lower prices. However, it pays to watch the Weather Channel in the days leading up your vacation, especially if you're traveling late August through early October, peak hurricane period.

By Caribbean standards, the Grenadines receive relatively little rain, particularly during the dry season—roughly November through April—when these small islands appear increasingly brown and scrubby. Water is supplied solely by cisterns and desalination plants (taking shorter showers and using fewer towels reduces our impact). Usually by July, the Grenadines start to take on a cloak of green, and they can look downright lush in October. By contrast, Grenada and

St. Vincent—being more mountainous—are more verdant, and dense rain forests climb the slopes from as low as a few hundred feet above sea level. Rain is frequent in the higher elevations (150 inches annually inland on St. Vincent, for instance), although along the coasts and other low-lying areas, showers tend to be brief (80 inches along the coast of St. Vincent).

Summer, while only about five degrees hotter than winter, feels much warmer due to the increased humidity and decreased wind. The one constant is the sun. It is always strong and will swiftly fry unprotected pale faces—and bodies—to a glowing shade of lobster red.

Building a Base for Tanning

Since the advent of tanning machines, pretanning accelerators, sunless tanning creams, and "mist-on" tanning, there is absolutely no reason to get burned on your first day out in the tropical sun. With some advance attention, you can stay outside for hours on your first day, and let's face it, what you want to do when you step off the plane is hit the beach.

Just about every town has a tanning center (we here at Rum & Reggae just call them "fake 'n bake" or "Playa Electrica"). Most health clubs have one or two tanning beds lying around, beckoning pasty skins to look healthier and more attractive in a matter of minutes. Ultraviolet tanning is relatively safe when used properly, because the UVB light doesn't have the severe burning rays of earlier sun lamps or, of course, the sun.

Pretan accelerators, available from a wide variety of manufacturers, chemically stimulate the manufacture of melanin, the pigment that darkens your skin. (Normally it takes direct exposure to the sun to start its production.) A pretan accelerator doesn't change your color or dye your skin. Rather, it prepares the skin with extra melanin so that you tan the first time out rather than burn, and much faster, too.

Sunless tanning creams, also available from a wide variety of manufacturers, use the chemical DHA to oxidize the natural proteins in the skin. Unlike the orange-staining QT of yesteryear (whoops, we're dating ourselves!), this creates an authentic tan, all without harmful UV rays. The only downside is the evenness of the tan, which depends on the application of the cream. Streaking can occur with this method.

We personally prefer "mist-on" tanning, a mechanically or technician-applied misting process using a combination of bronzer and sunless tanning creams. The bronzer provides the instant tan, and gradually fades into the real tan that comes with the misted-on tanning creams. The advantage of the "mist-on" technique is the evenness of the tan when compared to other methods. Just be sure to follow directions and don't wear white for the first day!

What to Wear and Take Along

Less is more. That is always the motto to remember when packing to go to the Caribbean. Bring only what you can carry for 10 minutes at a good clip, because you'll often be schlepping your luggage for at least that time, and it's hot. If you haven't already done so, invest in a piece of luggage with wheels.

What you really need to take along are a bathing suit, shorts, T-shirts or tanks, cotton sweater, a pair of sandals, sunglasses, and a Discman or iPod. After all, you are on vacation. However, this is the new millennium and people are dressing up for no reason, so you may want to bring some extra togs to look presentable at the dinner table. To help you be totally prepared (and to make your packing a lot easier), we've assembled a list of essentials for a week.

The Packing List

Clothes

- [ ] bathing suit (or two)
- [ ] T-shirts (4) — you'll end up buying at least one
- [ ] tank tops (2) — they're cooler, show off your muscles or curves, and even out T-shirt tan lines
- [ ] polo shirts (2)

The Grenadines (including St. Vincent and Grenada) Superlatives ⊛

Best Large Luxury Resort (over 50 rooms)	**Carenage Bay**, Canouan
Best Small Luxury Resort (under 50 rooms)	**Cotton House**, Mustique
Best Resort for Kids	**Grenada Grand Beach Resort**, Grenada
Best Romantic Hotel	**Petit St. Vincent**
Best Boutique Hotel	**Laluna**, Grenada
Best Inn	**The Frangipani**, Bequia
Best Eco-Friendly "Green" Hotel	**La Sagesse**, Grenada
Best Guest House	**Julie's**, Bequia
Best Room with a View	**Caribbee Inn**, Carriacou
Best Continental Restaurant	**Le Petit Jardin**, Bequia
Best Caribbean-Fusion Restaurant	**Firefly**, Mustique
Best Steak and Seafood Restaurant	**The Lime**, St. Vincent
Best Italian Restaurant	**Palapa**, Canouan
Best Vegetarian Restaurant	**La Sagesse**, Grenada
Best Lunch Spot	**Aquarium**, Grenada
Best Sunday Brunch	**Cotton House**, Mustique
Best Rum Punch	**Morne Fendue Plantation House**, Grenada
Best Place for a Sunset Cocktail	**Da Reef**, Bequia
Best Nightclub	**Fantazia 2001**, Grenada
Best Place for Nightlife	**St. George's**, Grenada
Best Place for Celebrity Spotting	**Firefly**, Mustique
Best Carnival	**Carriacou**
Best Music Festival	**Mustique Blues Festival**, Mustique
Best Diving	**Mayreau Gardens**, Mayreau
Best Snorkeling	**Tobago Cays**
Best Golf Course	**Carenage Bay**, Canouan
Best Hike	**La Soufriere**, St. Vincent
Best Waterfall	**Trinity Falls**, St. Vincent
Best Tennis	**Carenage Bay**, Canouan
Best Spa	**Cotton House**, Mustique
Best Shopping	**The Saturday marketplace in St. George's**, Grenada
Best T-shirt	**Jack Iron Strong Rum**, Carriacou
Best Value	**Bequia**
Best-Kept Secret	**Mayreau**

- [ ] shorts (2)
- [ ] nice, compatible lightweight pants (also good for the plane)
- [ ] sandals — those that can get wet, like Tevas, are best
- [ ] cotton sweater or sweatshirt
- [ ] undergarments
- [ ] sneakers (or good walking shoes) or topsiders (for boaters)

Women: lightweight dress (most women prefer to bring a couple of dresses for evening)

Men: if you must have a lightweight sport coat, wear it (with appropriate shoes) on the plane

Essentials

- [ ] toiletries and any necessary meds
- [ ] sunscreens (SPF 15+, 8, 4 [oil], and lip protector)
- [ ] moisturizers
- [ ] pure aloe gel for sunburn
- [ ] some good books — don't count on finding a worthwhile read there
- [ ] Cutter's or Woodsman's insect repellent, or Skin So Soft (oh, those nasty bugs)
- [ ] sunglasses (we bring two pairs!)
- [ ] hat or visor!
- [ ] Discman (CDs) or iPod
- [ ] camcorder, digital camera, or pocket camera (disposables are great for the beach and underwater disposables for snorkeling)

Sports Accessories (where applicable)

- [ ] tennis racquet
- [ ] golf clubs
- [ ] hiking shoes
- [ ] fins, mask, snorkel, regulator, and C-card (certification card)

And...

☐ ATM card and credit cards

☐ valid passport (keep in hotel safe and carry around a photocopy in your wallet)

☐ driver's license

The 12 Best Beaches in the Grenadines, St. Vincent, and Grenada

All kinds of beaches are found in these islands. There are beautiful strands on uninhabited outposts, as well as coves that are kept immaculate by tony resorts. Only St. Vincent comes up short in this department, although there are several gorgeous black-sand beaches found in remote areas.

Lower Bay — Bequia

The vibe here is almost always smooth and relaxing, the swimming is bliss and the beach bars will prepare a lobster while you sun. If things get too busy you can make the ten-minute hike over the hill to undeveloped Princess Margaret Beach.

Anse la Roche — Carriacou

This little charmer is tucked away on the north end of the island, reached only by dirt road and a short hike. It's worth it, and you may be the only one enjoying its unspoiled beauty.

Carenage Bay — Canouan

This superb cove now has a ritzy resort rising behind it, but it's an excellent place for swimming, and the three-mile-long reef that protects it from Atlantic breakers offers scintillating snorkeling.

Grand Anse — Grenada

This is the longest and liveliest beach in these islands — two miles in length. Although there are a couple big resorts (and several smaller ones), Grand Anse never seems overwhelmed by the development, and the view into Grenada's pretty mountains and downtown harbor is usually splendid.

Levera — Grenada

Enjoy this one while it lasts. A major hotel and golf development is underway for this area, and we're not clear on what it means to this fine, inverted curl of sand that faces the tiniest and most southerly Grenadines. You'll need to ask for directions.

Pink Gin — Grenada

Another hotel beach, but this one stops and starts over a stretch of about a mile, and midway is a terrific beach restaurant, the Aquarium. You'll find a spot of your own.

Saltwhistle Bay — Mayreau

It takes some effort to get here (there's not even an airport on this island), but this perfect crescent of sand is shallow and soothing and uncrowded. There's also a "matching" beach on the Atlantic side that — although not ideal for swimming — is great for walks.

Macaroni — Mustique

This is our favorite place for a picnic, and you might be sharing the sand with one of the notables that vacation here. The undertow can be tricky, however, so use caution when swimming.

Casuarina — Palm Island

This beach caters to guests of the resort, but is open to all, including day sail visitors. The beach bar is, thankfully, open to all, too.

Petit St. Vincent — Petit St. Vincent

Although all these beaches are open to the public, this privately owned island can probably guarantee more seclusion than just about any other hotel beach in these islands. The sand is soft, the reefs are good for snorkeling, and the resort gently coddles its guests with creature comforts — drink, lunch, cool water, towels, and showers.

Wallilabou — St. Vincent

This ebony beauty is deep and sexy and, except for a small

restaurant, pretty well undeveloped. It's our favorite water-side hangout on this undiscovered island.

Tobago Cays

There are five of these little uninhabited islets, and they've been totally discovered by the yachties, but they are undeniably lovely and offer super snorkeling in crystalline waters.

About Money

The Eastern Caribbean dollar—widely referred to as "EC"—is the official currency of both St. Vincent and the Grenadines and Grenada. With the exception of hotel rate cards, prices are usually represented in EC dollars, but it never hurts to check, especially with taxi drivers. The exchange rate is fixed to the U.S. dollar at a rate of EC$2.68 = US$1. All prices in this book have been converted to U.S. dollars.

Because the rate of the EC is fixed, U.S. dollars are accepted throughout these islands, but usually the exchange rate is rounded off to 2.50 for one U.S. dollar (you'll get a better exchange rate using most credit cards). The result is that, if you pay with greenbacks for ferry rides, taxi transfers, souvenir stands, and other cash-only purchases, by the end of your vacation you will have been nickled-and-dimed, perhaps by hundreds of dollars. Our advice: Go to a local bank at the start of your trip (found on every island except Palm, Petit St. Vincent, and Mayreau) and exchange US$ for EC$. Most (if not all) banks do not charge a commission.

Rum & Reggae Punch

Are you dreaming of the tropics, but it's snowing outside? Don't worry, you can create your own heat with this recipe.

Ingredients

1 lime
4 oz. water
2–3 oz. good dark rum (the stronger, the better)
2 oz. sugar syrup*
bitters
ice
freshly grated nutmeg

Directions

Squeeze the lime and add the juice and water to the rum and sugar syrup in a tall glass. Shake bitters into the glass four times. Add the rocks, then sprinkle with freshly grated nutmeg (it must be fresh!). Yum! Serves one.

* To make sugar syrup, combine 1 lb. sugar and 2 cups of water in a saucepan. Boil for about 2 minutes for sugar to dissolve. Let cool. Keep handy for quick and easy rum punches.

The Grenadines

The 75-mile-long chain of islands strung between St. Vincent and Grenada, the Grenadines, is a yachters' dream — second only to the British Virgin Islands as the Caribbean's prime sailing destination. There are more than 25 islands in the archipelago; most are uninhabited and can be explored on day trips, providing great opportunities for snorkeling, scuba diving, beach-combing, and picnics.

The islands belong to two countries: St. Vincent and the Grenadines are one, and Grenada is the other. Seven of the islands are home to some of the most amazing resorts in the Caribbean. The first of the major islands encountered heading south from St. Vincent is Bequia, the second most populated of the Grenadines and perhaps the most captivating. Next is Mustique, home of the rich, famous, and fabulous; Canouan, the location of the first megaresort in the Grenadines; Mayreau, still a real gem and another favorite; Union Island, spectacular from a distance, a bit boring up close; Palm Island, where a classic hideaway has been revitalized; and Petit St. Vincent, or PSV, a truly private old-money getaway. Just beyond PSV is a popular stop on the cruising circuit, the unpopulated Tobago Cays, a mini-archipelago of five tiny islets with great beaches and snorkeling (lots of boats will be anchored offshore). Continuing south, the Grenadian border is crossed upon reaching Petite Martinique, aka PM, the reputed smuggling capital of the West Indies. Next is Carriacou, the largest of

the Grenadines but a true step back in time. Finally, there is the island of Grenada, signaling the southern conclusion of the chain.

Bequia, Carriacou, and Mustique are in "The Larger Grenadines"
section of the book. Canouan, Mayreau, Union, Petite Martinique,
Palm Island and Petit St. Vincent—are covered in "The Smaller
Grenadines." St. Vincent and Grenada, the much bigger north and
south "anchor" islands of the Grenadines and the two governing
bodies of this archipelago, have their own chapters at the end of
the book.

Getting There

Because the Grenadines are smaller islands, they don't have large air-
ports, and therefore you'll need to reach them via connecting flights
from their larger neighbors. This inconvenience has a payoff: Development in the Grenadines has stayed small and low-scale while
many other Caribbean islands have sold their souls to cement mixers
and back hoes. So yes, you'll spend a little more time getting to the
Grenadines, but we think the extra effort has a payoff.

Most people reach the Grenadines and St. Vincent via Barbados,
about 100 miles (about 160 km) to the east (like Barbados, Grenada
is served by flights from outside the Caribbean—see that chapter for
details). Barbados is served by **Air Jamaica, American, American Eagle,
BWIA,** and **US Airways** from the U.S.; by **Air Canada** and **BWIA**
from Toronto; and by **British Airways, BWIA,** and **Virgin Atlantic** from
London. Once in Barbados, it's a one-hour flight to the Grenadines
using **Mustique Airways** (800-526-4789 or 784-458-4380; www.mus-
tiqueairways.com), **SVG Air** (866-678-4247 or 784-457-5124; www.-
svgair.com) or Barbados-based **TIA** (246-418-1654; www.TIA-
2000.com)—see the respective chapters for flight details. The
government of St. Vincent and the Grenadines maintains a small
tourism desk at the Barbados airport that is open from about 1 p.m.
until the last flight to the Grenadines departs. The staff at the desk
can assist with connections and hotel reservations. Alas, many North
American residents cannot make it to the Grenadines in one day, so
an overnight in Barbados may be necessary. There are many lodging

possibilities on bustling Barbados, the best of which are outlined in *Rum & Reggae's Caribbean* guidebook (available from www.rumreggae.com). Most are at least a 30-minute drive from the airport, but one that works particularly well for in-transit travelers on a budget is suggested below.

Peach and Quiet, Inch Marlow, Christ Church, Barbados, W.I.
  🕐 246-428-5682, ✉ 246-428-2467,
  💻 www.peachandquiet.com

⑤ **Cheap** 🍴 **EP** (cc)

While we think the moniker is W.T.Q. (Way Too Queer), this small hotel is located in better-named Inch Marlow, a residential area a half-mile south of the Barbados airport. The spot is a world away from hustle and noise of the island's busier districts, and you won't hear planes landing. The seaside inn's secret is a minimalist approach to infrastructure—some of which needs cosmetic work—but the reception is unstinting. So, although there's no bartender, the installation of an honor bar means drinks cost under $2; and although Inch Marlow is not near dining, taxi vans sponsored by several fine restaurants shuttle guests two nights a week, minimizing the need for a rental car. Rooms are basic but have quality bedding; do note that there's no air conditioning, TV, or phones. The owners serve tasty meals, there's a deep pool, and the beach is a five-minute walk. Walking tours of the island are a specialty.

Other connections into the Grenadines are possible via Martinique, St. Lucia, Trinidad—all discussed in *Rum & Reggae's Caribbean* guidebook (available from www.rumreggae.com)—and of course Grenada, which is covered in this book. It's also possible to use the ferry services that run from St. Vincent south to Union, and from Grenada north to Carriacou and Petite Martinique. Details on the ferries are listed in each respective chapter. Crossing the border between the two countries is most easily accomplished using the smaller airlines listed above, although water taxis can be hired on Union and Carriacou.

The Larger
Grenadines

Bequia

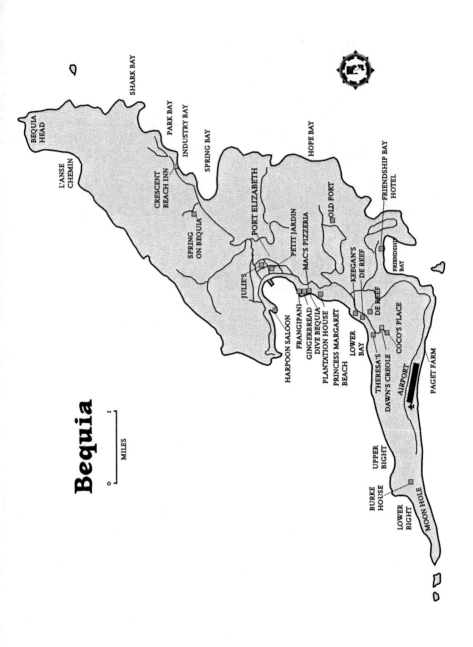

MILES

BEQUIA HEAD

L'ANSE CHEMIN

SHARK BAY

PARK BAY

INDUSTRY BAY

SPRING BAY

CRESCENT BEACH INN

SPRING ON BEQUIA

PORT ELIZABETH

HOPE BAY

PETIT JARDIN

MAC'S PIZZERIA

OLD FORT

JULIE'S

KEEGAN'S

DE REEF

FRIENDSHIP BAY HOTEL

HARPOON SALOON

FRANGIPANI

GINGERBREAD

DIVE BEQUIA

PLANTATION HOUSE

PRINCESS MARGARET BEACH

LOWER BAY

DE REEF

FRIENDSHIP BAY

COCO'S PLACE

THERESA'S

DAWN'S CREOLE

AIRPORT

PAGET FARM

UPPER BIGHT

BURKE HOUSE

LOWER BIGHT

MOON HOLE

Bequia

SITTING AT THE BAR AT THE FRANGIPANI ENJOYING A "Happy" Hairoun, the Vincentian brew, on our first visit to Bequia (pronounced "BECK-wee") way back in 1987, we unwittingly revealed to the woman next to us that we were travel writers. She stiffened and brusquely requested that we not write anything about Bequia. "We don't need or want any more tourists," she said with conviction. It's the typical response of a seasonal resident who wants to slam the door in the face of any new arrival, but as we got to know Bequia, the northernmost of the Grenadines, we began to agree with her. This island is extraordinary—we would hate to see it spoiled. So it was with great reluctance and profuse apologies that we brought Bequia to light in the first edition of *Rum & Reggae* (1988). After all these years, it still relatively unspoiled and has managed to retain its magical charm.

The best way to describe Bequia is as the quintessential Caribbean experience—a harmony of all the elements that make the islands special. It is pretty, clean, and small enough to get to know intimately. The local residents are very friendly and responsive. There are handsome beaches, good restaurants, lots of bars, shops, and accommodations that are very reasonably priced. A sea orientation and a yachty element add the perfect touch to the island's ambiance.

For such a small place, Bequia is surprisingly lively. It's easy to spend a week here and not be bored. The action revolves around the waterfront of Port Elizabeth, starting at the ferry dock and winding around the Belmont Walkway to Princess Margaret Beach (also known as Tony Gibbons Beach). Here you can browse in a small but intelligent bookshop, buy some fresh fruit and vegetables from Rastas, have a few drinks, check out the brown coral jewelry displayed by sidewalk vendors, dance to pan music, eat lobster pizza, go scuba

Bequia: Key Facts

Location	13°N by 60°W 9 miles (15 km) south of St. Vincent 2,050 miles (3,299 km) southeast of New York
Size	7 square miles (11 square km) 5 miles (8 km) long by 3 miles (5 km) wide
Highest point	Belle Pointe, 881 feet (269 m)
Population	4,874
Language	English
Time	Atlantic Standard Time (1 hour ahead of EST, same as EDT)
Area code	784
Electricity	220 volts AC, 50 cycles, so you'll need an adapter and transformer
Currency	The Eastern Caribbean dollar, EC$ (EC$2.68 = US $1)
Driving	On the LEFT; you'll need a temporary permit, which costs $28 — just present your valid U.S. or Canadian driver's license and pay the fee
Documents	Proof of citizenship (we recommend a valid passport) and a return or ongoing ticket
Departure tax	$13
Beer to drink	Hairoun
Rum to drink	Any Vincentian brand
Music to hear	Dancehall
Tourism info	On-island: 784-458-3286; in New York: 800-729-1726 www.bequiatourism.com

diving, buy clothes and T-shirts, have more drinks, and go for a swim at a pretty beach — all in a half-mile stretch.

Bequia has a great mix of people, too. In addition to the welcoming locals, there are all kinds of interesting visitors. The island has always attracted an artsy element. The late Sanford Meisner, the famed acting teacher, maintained a house here and often conducted classes and seminars on Bequia. Many artists spend the winter here, finding more than enough inspiration from the surroundings. There are lots of Europeans, especially Germans, who seem to love the island's mellow pace. The North Americans who visit tend to be more sophisticated (if less demanding) than, say, the average tourists who go to Aruba. Bequia appeals to independent travelers (readers, that's you) who are looking for a low-key yet stimulating environment to shake off and forget whatever pressures they have in their everyday worlds. Finally, there are the boat people—the cocktail cruisers who come in on their yachts or charter boats and love to have a good time. They add a little zip and glamour to the mix.

There have been a few changes on Bequia over the last decade. The most anticipated was the opening of the airport near Paget Farm in 1992. Built with a grant from the European Community, it made getting here in one day possible from both North America and Europe. Thankfully, fears of hordes of tourists overrunning the island never materialized. The airport's convenience is appreciated by all except the residents of Moon Hole (the planes often fly overhead when making their approach). Unwelcome by most locals and repeat visitors was the inclusion of Bequia on the itineraries of several smaller cruise ships. The airport didn't overwhelm, but the cruise ships disgorge souvenir-hunting and bathroom-seeking passengers into town. Fortunately the former prime minister, who hails from Bequia, put some limits on arrivals to preserve the island's special character. Other changes here include the reclamation of the Belmont Walkway, which winds along Admiralty Bay and connects the waterfront shops, restaurants, and hotels from the center of town to the Plantation House Hotel. Where once ocean surge and boat wake used to pelt the protective seawall, there is now a few feet of beach. The walkway makes for a great stroll along the bay at sunset (cocktail in hand, of course). Bequia's old ferry schooner, the Friendship Rose, was refurbished and now makes day excursions to Mustique, the Tobago Cays, and other Grenadines. There's even a FedEx office—albeit a tiny one!

The Briefest History

Not much is known about Amerindian settlements on Bequia until the 1600s, when the Caribs inhabited an island they called Becouya, which means "Island of the Clouds" (a strange name for this rather dry island — perhaps it was rainy on the day it was named). There is no record of Columbus sighting the island on any of his voyages. Bequia was left in peace by the warring European navies in the region. Then in 1675, the slave ship Palmira sank off the island, and some of the slaves on board escaped and were welcomed by the Caribs. As a result of the intermarriage between Caribs and runaway African slaves, the tribe became known as Black Caribs. They used Bequia as a staging port for attacks on the Yellow Caribs of St. Vincent. The French soon claimed the settlement and all of the Grenadines. The French also imported slaves, many of whom escaped and went into St. Vincent's mountains and joined the Black Caribs. The result was too many headaches and battles with the Black Caribs for the French, so the islands were declared neutral between France and Britain in the Treaty of Aix-la-Chapelle in 1748. Of course, treaties were meant to be broken, and the two battled it out until finally, in 1783, the Treaty of Versailles deeded the islands to the British. One last gasp by the allied forces of the Black Caribs and the French failed to dislodge the British, and most of the Black Caribs were shipped off to Roatan (near Honduras). In 1871 the islands became a part of the British Windward Islands, and in 1979 St. Vincent and the Grenadines achieved independent statehood within the British Commonwealth.

Getting There

Bequia's major gateway is Barbados, which lies about 100 miles to the east. Once in Barbados, connect to **Mustique Airways** or **SVG Air** for the 55-minute flight to Bequia.

Alternatively, fly to St. Vincent on **BWIA**, **Caribbean Star** or **LIAT** from one of the neighboring islands. Once on St. Vincent, you can either fly on to Bequia (via Mustique or SVG) or take a short taxi ride to the ferry dock in Kingstown and ride over on one of the small ships that ply the Grenadines. There are up to eight ferries a day making the trip, the fare is a bargain $6, and the one-hour crossing is just long enough to be enjoyable but not so long as to induce seasickness. Departure times change, so check with the tourist office for exact schedules (784-458-3286). You can also take the MV Barracuda, a mail boat that travels southbound through the Grenadines on Monday and Thursday mornings, northbound on Tuesday and Friday.

Getting Around

Bequia is a small island, and you can walk everywhere if you like exercise. However, there are some hills to climb and descend to get to the other side, so you may want to take a taxi, which your hotel can call for you. Other options are the public minivans that ply the main roads (fares are $1 almost anywhere), or your thumb. There are three car-rental agencies on the island: **B&G Jeep Rental** (784-458-3760), **Phil's Car Rental** (784-458-3304), and **Sunset View Rental** (784-457-3558). Prices are a bit steep—averaging about $50 for a day—but lower rates are available for longer rentals, and you can sometimes wheel and deal in the off-season. You can also rent a bike from the **Lighthouse** (784-458-3084). Water taxis will take you from town or the Frangipani dock to Princess Margaret Beach or Lower Bay for $5.

Focus on Bequia: Exploring the Magic

It's easy to become possessive about Bequia because it is a small island that can easily become familiar in a week's time. After discovering the magic of this island, you begin to feel that it's your own. So definitely get out and see it. There are walks that will take you to just about anywhere on the island in an hour or less. Port Elizabeth, where most of the hotels are, is not only the island's hub but its center as well—all roads lead to town. The walks are fairly easy, up over the hills to the other side.

Our favorite walk is to Industry, although the name is a misnomer if ever there was one. Leaving town on the road to Spring, you will climb over the hill and come upon an old sugar mill ruin, overgrown with hibiscus and bougainvillea, on the left—a good photo op. It is then a pleasant walk through tall coconut trees, acres of them, with the usually deserted Spring beach off to the right. The road follows the curve of a bluff, offering terrific views of Petit Nevis and Mustique. It quietly descends into more coconut groves and Industry Beach.

There is a bar at the Crescent Beach Inn where you can quaff a rum punch before heading back, and the swimming here is also good.

Or continue on a little farther to Orton "Brother" King's Oldhegg Turtle Sanctuary in Park Bay. King started the sanctuary in 1995 to raise endangered Hawksbill hatchlings brought to him from neighboring islands. His facility houses turtles until they are three years old, when they are released into the sea—more than 500 to date. A $5 donation is suggested. For the industrious, there is a hike from here to Bequia Head on cow paths. This should be attempted only with ample daylight. People get lost, so be sure of the way back and wear good walking shoes.

Another area worth exploring is Moon Hole, an innovative development on the western end of Bequia. Designed and built by the late Tom Johnston starting in the 1960s, it strives to blend with its natural surroundings, and to a great degree it succeeds. The stone used in the walls matches the cliffs and gullies where they are built, and a lot of the construction is actually poured concrete. At first sight it looks as though the developer ran out of money. The complex looks unfinished; there is no glass in the window, no color except for gray stone and metal. Yet that is the architect's intention—to achieve harmony with the striking natural setting. The centerpiece of this creation is Moon Hole, a huge natural arch that, it is said, frames the full moon. Underneath the arch is a terrace and a wood and stone house that hasn't been used in many years (due to falling rocks from the arch). It is weather beaten and dilapidated but still adorned with relics from when Tom Johnston and his wife lived there (it is the first house they built). It's a bit odd but still stunning. To get to Moon Hole, take the road to Friendship and at the top of the hill follow the right fork (the left takes you down to the Friendship Bay Hotel). The road will hug the coast through La Pompe and Paget Farm. You'll pass Bequia's airport. Keep going and you'll eventually reach the entrance to Moon Hole. Be as discreet as the designers were—this is not meant to be a tourist attraction.

A third walk takes you to Hope Bay and a totally deserted beach that is perfect for nude sunbathing. For this one, you'll want to take a taxi to the Old Fort Country Inn and arrange for a pickup later on.

Bring water and refreshment, as it is a long way down the mountain and a hot way back up. The friendly folks at the inn will direct you to the path. Sit and have a rum punch to get ready for the trip, and then off you go. The trail is not difficult, but you will sweat a little. Once at the beach, be careful swimming as the water can be rough. If you want privacy, there is the ruin of an old mill on the north side of the beach, which is perfect for some hanky-panky if you are so inclined. When you return, be sure to have another rum punch as your reward for a job well done.

If you want to explore what's under the water, there is **Dive Bequia** (800-525-3833 or 784-458-3504; www.dive-bequia.com). This is a very laid-back operation in the most "for sure" Southern California style. Run by Bob Sachs, Dive Bequia offers anything from snorkel trips, resort courses, and PADI certification to night dives and underwater videos of yourself doing a Lloyd Bridges imitation. Bob has great T-shirts for sale, too. The other dive shops on the island are **Dive Paradise** (784-458-3563), **Friendship Bay Dive Resort** (784-457-3333), and **Bequia Dive Adventures** (784-458-3247), all of which offer boat dives, equipment rental, NAUI or PADI certification, snorkeling, and sailing trips. Certainly one of them will satisfy any "Sea Hunt" urges.

Where to Stay

There are a few more options for staying on Bequia these days. Most are very reasonably priced and quite satisfactory. Prices on Bequia are still much lower than on the more tourist-oriented islands. So who's complaining?

⊛**The Frangipani**, P.O. Box 1, Bequia, St. Vincent and the Grenadines, W.I. ℭ Stateside: 800-525-3833, Local: 784-458-3255, ✎ 784-458-3824, 🖳 www.frangipanibequia.com, frangi@caribsurf.com

　　💲 **Cheap** for the main house, **Not So Cheap** for the Garden Units, and **Pricey** for the Deluxe rooms 🍴 **EP** **CC**

　　Always a favorite place of ours, the Frangi (as it is affectionately called) is our first choice for accommodations on Bequia.

Owned by the prime minister of St. Vincent and The Grenadines, Sir James, and "Son" Mitchell, and well run and maintained by manager Sabrina Mitchell, the Frangipani sits on a
point in the middle of the Belmont Walkway and seems to be
the hub of the island. Because it is the center of attention, especially with the yachty set, there are people either marching
by or sitting at its busy bar all day long. It's just a social kind
of place. The old main house, with its trademark red roof, has
several rooms with shared cold-water bathrooms and furnished with mahogany antiques. The newer Traditional and
Garden rooms are made of stone and wood; they are much
larger, more spacious, and private and have sun decks. The
Garden rooms are bigger and more deluxe and have terrific
views of the harbor. On Thursday nights, there is a barbecue
and buffet with decent pan bands for jump-up. Get there
early because the music stops around 11 p.m., as does most
activity on Bequia. The Frangi also has a 44-foot cutter (sailboat) called the Pelangi, which is available for day ($200 per
day for up to four) or multiday charters.

The Plantation House Hotel, P.O. Box 16, Admiralty Bay, Bequia,
St. Vincent and the Grenadines, W.I. ⓒ 784-458-3425,
🕾 784-458-3612, 🖳 www.hotel-plantation.com, info@hotel-
plantation.com

💲 **Very Pricey** 🍴 **CP** ⓒ🄲

Ideally situated between a stellar beach and the diversion of
the waterfront, this is the most expensive place to stay on Bequia. The establishment, a symphony of pink and turquoise,
offers two choices for lodging: five rooms in the main house
and 22 cabanas dotting the grounds. The cabanas, especially
those around the coconut tree-studded common, offer the
most room and privacy. Each cabana has a small veranda,
ceiling fan, air conditioning, satellite TV, phone, and fridge.

However, the Plantation House has seen better days and
could use a face-lift — particularly the room furnishings. Our
twin beds sagged, and the pillows were as fluffy as a sack of

flour. At these rates, we expect to sleep comfortably. The main house has a wraparound arched veranda where meals are served and which we also found disappointing (especially breakfast), considering the plethora of good dining options on Bequia. Fortunately the manicured grounds are lush and pleasant, so sipping a cocktail in the shade of a palm tree assuages some of the hotel's deficiencies. There is a small but attractive, raised kidney-shaped pool along with the Greenflash Bar & Restaurant at the water's edge. A tiny beach with chaise lounges is tucked in front of the bar, but it's worth the five-minute walk over the point to H.R.H. Maggie's Beach. The Plantation House hosts a popular barbecue night on Tuesdays at the Greenflash, replete with a reggae-soca band.

⊛ **Julie's Guest House,** P.O. Box 12, Port Elizabeth, Bequia, St. Vincent and the Grenadines, W.I. ✆ 784-458-3304, 🖂 784-458-3812, 💻 julies@caribsurf.com

💲 **Cheap** and up 🍴 **MAP** (an EP rate is also available) **CC**

Julie's is still one of the best deals in the Caribbean. For $39 a single, $65 a double, you get a room *with* breakfast and dinner. The 21 rooms are very simple, with firm platform double beds, mosquito nets, blond wood, bright wall colors, newly tiled floors, and private baths (all the rooms in the front building now have hot water). The food is good West Indian fare and, again, very simple. You really enjoy the meals here because the whole place is such a bargain that the food seems *free*.

Julie's is not on the beach; it's one block in from the harbor in a residential neighborhood. You'll hear dogs barking and roosters crowing at all times (especially as you try to fall asleep). The "lullaby of Bequia" usually starts in the middle of the night with either an all-dog or an all-rooster chorus. They sing a duet that builds to a cacophony and then gradually winds down. You get used to it.

The people who stay here are an interesting bunch and are usually repeaters. This is not a place to be antisocial. There is a bar where a bunch of Julie's friends listen to the cricket matches. The staff is courteous and very friendly, especially when you introduce yourself.

Keegan's Guest House and Apartments, Lower Bay, Bequia, St. Vincent and the Grenadines, W.I. ✆ 784-458-3530, ✉ 784-457-3313, 💻 www.keegansbequia.com, keegansbequia@yahoo.com

💲 **Cheap** 🍴 **MAP** (guest house), **EP** (apartments), credit cards are not accepted.

Another great Bequia deal, this is your best bet if you want cheap accommodations at the beach with meals. Keegan's is an 11-room guest house less than 100 yards from a great and really fun beach, Lower Bay. Being a guest house, it has very simple rooms, but they do have private baths, ceiling fans, and mosquito nets. The newer apartments, located just across the street from the Lower Bay beach and De Reef Bar & Restaurant, are also a great value. These spacious units are decently furnished and feature private baths and fully equipped kitchens. Keegan's restaurant serves good West Indian fare, and there are several other options right in Lower Bay.

The Old Fort Country Inn, Mount Pleasant, Bequia, St. Vincent and the Grenadines, W.I. ✆ 784-458-3440, ✉ 784-457-3340, 💻 www.theoldfort.com, info@theoldfort.com

💲 **Not So Cheap** to **Pricey** 🍴 **EP** CC

Situated on 30 acres on top of the very breezy mount, the Old Fort commands the best views of any establishment on Bequia. Working with the remains of an old mill, this is a wonderfully peaceful environment, often accented by classical music. Both the common areas and the guest rooms have the original stone walls and natural woods. The parlor even has a fireplace for those occasional cool nights on the hilltop. The six rooms are simply but comfortably furnished, and the lanai of room 5 is one of the best places to read a book while the view and the breeze provide welcome distraction. Since the beach is a hike away, there is a large pool for cooling off. The Old

Fort has an excellent Mediterranean-Creole restaurant, and it's also a great site for small groups and conferences.

Spring on Bequia, Spring Bay, Bequia, St. Vincent and the Grenadines, W.I. (P.O. Box 19251, Minneapolis, MN 55419), ⓒ Stateside: 612-823-1202, Local: 784-458-3414, 🕸 784-457-3305, 🖳 www.springonbequia.com, candy@springonbequia.com

🛄 **Not So Cheap** 🕦 **EP** (add $45 per day per person for MAP); ⒸⒸ Closed from mid-June through October.

If you want real quiet (i.e., seclusion) with extraordinary views, stay at Spring. Situated on a hillside amid the ruins of an old sugar mill and acres of coconut palms, this is one of the most peaceful (some might call it dead) places to stay anywhere. The airy design of stone and wood blends wonderfully with the surroundings. This is a reader's and meditator's heaven. The rooms are simple and minimally furnished, yet they're comfortable and consistent with the tranquillity of this inn. Most have views of the uninhabited islands of Baliceaux and Battowia from their lanais. There is a restaurant serving all meals, including a very popular Sunday curry brunch (reservations necessary). A pretty pool and a clay tennis court are on the grounds for your leisure, and the wonderful walks and beaches of Spring and Industry are steps away.

The Gingerbread Hotel, P.O. Box 1, Bequia, St. Vincent and the Grenadines, W.I. ⓒ 784-458-3800, 🕸 784-458-3907, 🖳 www.gingerbreadhotel.com, ginger@caribsurf.com

🛄 **Not So Cheap** 🕦 ⒸⒸ

Right next to the Frangipani on Admiralty Bay and the Belmont Walkway is The Gingerbread. Long a popular restaurant, The Gingerbread opened its Bequia Suites in 1998. Like its namesake, quaintness abounds, with gingerbread-style buildings and manicured gardens surrounded by a stone wall. The latter provides a welcome sense of seclusion from the harbor hubbub. Suites come with a fully equipped kitchen, bath, adjoining salon, and large lanai. The upper-level suites have king-size beds smack dab in the middle of the room. The bed as the focal point of your vacation? Hey, not such a bad idea! The ground-level suites feature twin beds, and a third bed is available in each room ("Honey, do we have to bring the kids?"). The hotel has a beachside cafe, great for ice cream or java jive. The Gingerbread's restaurant is upstairs.

Crescent Beach Inn, Industry, Bequia, St. Vincent and the Grenadines, W.I. ✆ 784-458-3400

💰 **Cheap** ⑪ **CP** (no credit cards accepted)

We discovered this out-of-the-way place on a trip to Industry Bay. Set right on a deserted beach and completely surrounded by coconut palms, this is a spartan and very low-key kind of place. The three simple rooms flank a large pavilion with a bar and a Ping-Pong table. Breakfast comes with the package, but don't expect much more. If Zen is your style and hanging out on the beach, reading, or meditation is what you're into, this might work for you. If you need a ride into town, just ask Ricky (one of the owners)—he has a taxi business as well. The inn also has a fun Full-Moon Barbecue with live music held on...you guessed it.

Burke House, P.O. Box 1, Bequia, St. Vincent and the Grenadines, W.I. ✆ 784-457-3509, ✆ 784-458-3943, 🖥 www.begos.com/moonhole, consul@caribsurf.com

💰 About $3,000 per week (includes accommodations for four; r-t airfare from Barbados for two, rental vehicle, daily maid service/cook/laundress, and a food/drink allowance of $450 —a great deal!

This is a private home owned by John and Lusan Corbett (they live up the path in another house). Situated 100 feet above sea level in the famed (and restricted) Moon Hole development, this very secluded house was built in the 1960s by Tom Johnston. It's made of stone and purple heartwood and resembles something out of Bedrock (no glass in the windows). Vaulted stone ceilings enclose a living and dining-kitchen area and two bedrooms, each with bath (the master bath has one of the best views from the loo we've ever seen — talk about a nice place to contemplate!). Other views are spectacular, too, especially from the upper roof deck. To the north is volcanic St. Vincent, and to the south are fabulous Mustique and the Grenadine chain. There are no phones here, although 110-volt lighting and electricity have recently been installed. A hammock on the south terrace beckons, and a whalebone throne chair is available for the royalty among us. For about $25 a day, a maid (highly recommended) will cook, clean, do laundry, and bring provisions (which the renter pays for, of course). One of Bequia's prettiest and most deserted beaches is a two-minute walk from the house (it's the cover shot of this book!).

Where to Eat

Since the original edition of *Rum & Reggae*, there has been an explosion of restaurants on Bequia. If you're staying in town, avoid the hotel MAP plan because there are a number of good restaurants to experience. If you're staying at Spring or the Old Fort, the MAP plan makes sense because traveling for meals would be inconvenient (and you would spend a lot on cab fare). Here are our dining choices.

$$$ **Coco's Place**, Lower Bay, 784-458-3463
       Coco, a popular bartender, is the owner of this cool down-island pub and Bequian kitchen. Extensive à la carte and daily specials. He has satellite TV, live calypso on Fridays, live string band on Tuesdays, and Happy Hour from 6 to 7 p.m daily.

$$$ **Dawn's Creole Bar and Restaurant**, Lower Bay, 784-458-3154
       Located on a hill at the far end of Lower Bay, Dawn's serves excellent West Indian Creole cuisine and seafood specialties. Open for breakfast, lunch, and dinner, and a beach party is held on Sundays. Dinner reservations a must.

$$ ⊛ **De Reef**, Lower Bay, 784-458-3447
As you're already on the beach, this is a convenient and casual place for lunch and cocktails. Dinners here are surprisingly good.

$$$ **The Frangipani**, Port Elizabeth, 784-458-3255
At the hub of the Belmont Walkway, the Frangi has consistently served good Caribbean cuisine at very fair prices as long as we've been coming here. Reservations are suggested, especially for dinner.

$$$ **The Gingerbread**, Port Elizabeth, 784-458-3800
This is a Bequian institution, but the food is hardly institutional and is served in an airy second-floor dining room with views out onto the bay.

$$$ **Mac's Pizzeria and Bake Shop**, Port Elizabeth, 784-458-3474
Mac's is a must stop when on Bequia, if only for Mac's mouthwatering lobster pizza. Perched on the Belmont Walkway with a breezy veranda, and open for breakfast, lunch, and dinner. No stay on Bequia is complete without a pit stop here.

$$$$ **The Old Fort**, Mount Pleasant, 784-458-3440
Although things were in a state of flux during our most recent visit, the Old Fort has a reputation for delicious Creole and continental dishes in a very romantic and serene setting. An after-dinner stroll to stargaze is an added bonus that makes it worth the taxi ride up and back. Reservations are suggested.

$$$$$ ⊛ **Le Petit Jardin**, Port Elizabeth, 784-458-3318
Probably Bequia's most expensive restaurant, Le Petit Jardin is located off the beaten path on Back Street. But the cuisine, French with Creole flourishes, is excellent, as is the service. Reservations are suggested. Closed Sunday.

$$$ **Theresa's**, Lower Bay Beach, 784-458-3802
Located at the base of the hill in Lower Bay, Theresa will cook your own private Creole meal. You must call early in the day

for a dinner reservation, as everything is bought and prepared to order. Her Monday night international buffet is an island event not to be missed. No credit cards.

Don't Miss

Sailing the Grenadines

The nearby island of Mustique is a budget buster for most of us, but it's an enjoyable day trip aboard the Friendship Rose, an 80-foot wooden schooner that formerly served as a Grenadine mail boat. Calvin Lewis charges $60 for a seven-hour trip to Mustique, where you can bask on the beach in front of Mick Jagger's abode. Or journey to the idyllic and uninhabited Tobago Cays—the 10-hour trip costs $80, including lunch and snorkeling gear. Reservations: 784-458-3661.

Bequia Book Shop

Located on the waterfront across from the park, it features an excellent collection of West Indian writers and a good general selection. If it's maps and charts you're into, this is the place. Bequia Book Shop is owned by a very knowledgeable and polite ex-Bajan named Ian Gale, a good person to talk to about Caribbean authors. The store's logo T-shirt is a smart collector's item (as are the books).

Mac's Pizzeria

On Tuesday nights, Mac's throws a barbecue and jump-up with live bands.

Easter Regatta

This is a great time both on and off the race course, as the racing is meant to be fun rather than competitive.

Industry Bay

Be sure to see this part of the island. It boasts lofty palm groves, a secluded beach, and a spectacular view of several nearby islands.

De Reef

For drinks in Lower Bay; go on Sunday afternoons.

The Frangipani

For drinks at the hub, especially the Thursday night jump-ups.

The Harpoon Saloon

For sunset cocktails and a great view of the harbor. Also, their Saturday jump-ups are a blast.

Carriacou

TOURISTO SCALE

🐕 🐕 🐕

A FRIEND OF OURS ONCE TOLD US THAT JUST AS HER plane touched down on Carriacou (pronounced KARRY-a-coo), it suddenly lifted up with jarring swiftness. When she looked out the window, she saw a cow on the runway. That's Carriacou. It's on its own wavelength. Everyone — and everything — moves at its own pace (slow to slower), as did the runway keeper in this case. If you're an efficiency freak or into deluxe accommodations, this island isn't for you. What makes Carriacou special is its sense of detachment and the resulting preservation of some unique African and Caribbean customs.

The first inhabited island north of Grenada, Carriacou is the largest of the Grenadine chain, but it's still pretty small, at eight miles long and five miles wide. Most of its inhabitants live around the main village of Hillsborough. It gets extremely dry, almost parched, and as the winter progresses the island begins to look like autumn in New England — give or take a few palm trees and other tropical props. There are also several uninhabited "satellite islands" with gorgeous white-sand beaches.

After our first visit to Carriacou some years ago, we thought that an intrusion of tourism was around the corner, but that has not happened. There may be a few (small) cruise ships stopping here, taking advantage of idyllic Sandy Cay, but tourism on the island is mostly unchanged. As a matter of fact, things seem to have gone back in time. The only improvement in the last few years that we've noticed is that the airstrip is now fenced in, so there will be no more cows on the runway (and cars now have to make a long detour around the airstrip). Some of the roads have been repaired, although you'll still find stretches that are in abysmal shape. A few inns and guest

Carriacou

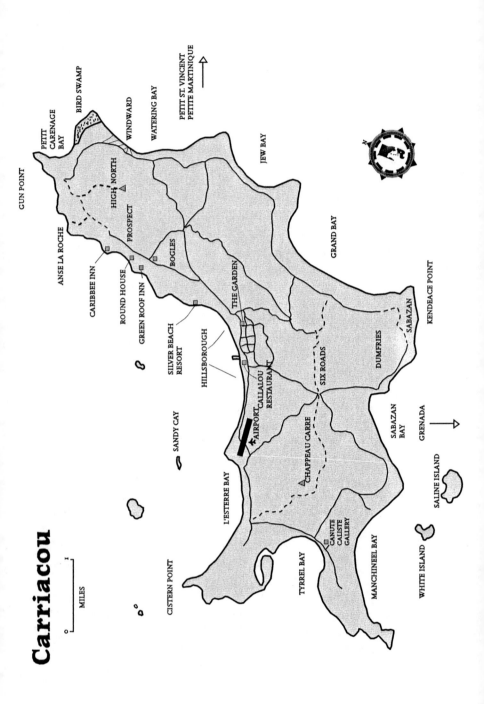

MILES

GUN POINT

PETIT CARENAGE BAY

BIRD SWAMP

WINDWARD

WATERING BAY

PETIT ST. VINCENT
PETITE MARTINIQUE

JEW BAY

ANSE LA ROCHE

HIGH NORTH

PROSPECT

CARIBBEE INN

ROUND HOUSE

GREEN ROOF INN

BOGLES

THE GARDEN

GRAND BAY

SILVER BEACH RESORT

HILLSBOROUGH

SANDY CAY

SABAZAN

KENDEACE POINT

SIX ROADS

DUMFRIES

AIRPORT

CALLALOU RESTAURANT

CHAPPEAU CARRE

SABAZAN BAY

GRENADA

L'ESTERRE BAY

SALINE ISLAND

CISTERN POINT

CANUTE CALISTE GALLERY

TYRREL BAY

MANCHINEEL BAY

WHITE ISLAND

houses have popped up, but nothing out of the ordinary. There was talk of an Italian conglomerate building a 200-room condo-hotel complex up on Windward Heights. We'll believe it when we see it! However, we once were skeptical about plans to develop another Grenadine, Canouan, and it did happen. So who knows? However, at this writing you can still get away from it all on Carriacou. There are enough people around to keep your sensibilities alive, and yet there is a mind-your-own-business philosophy—bred by the big business of smuggling—that allows you to socialize only when you want to do so. There are few formal activities designed for tourists.

The Briefest History

Carriacou is part of the country of Grenada, which achieved independence from Great Britain in 1974. During the 18th century the island was divided up into estates for raising sugarcane, and the lovely stone ruins of those plantations can be found around the island. The Kayaks (natives of Carriacou) are proud of their African heritage and take pains to preserve it. Both the English and the French colonialists left their marks in ways remarkable for such a small island. Most of the inhabitants of the town of Windward bear Scottish names, whereas those who live only a few miles away in L'Esterre have French names and still maintain a group (led by octogenarian artist Canute Caliste) that plays and dances the quadrille. Boat-building is still a major occupation, and Carriacou's sloops are rated among the best in the Caribbean.

Getting There

The main route to Carriacou is via Grenada on **SVG Air** along with less frequent service on **TIA** from Barbados. There are also ferries of modern and vintage persuasions, and these are a more appealing (and less expensive) way to travel. The **Osprey Express** (473-440-8126), a high-speed motor-catamaran, makes the trip in under 90 minutes. It departs from the Carenage in St. George's, Grenada, at 9 a.m. and

Carriacou: Key Facts

Location	12°N by 61°W
	23 miles (37 km) northeast of Grenada
	2,175 miles (3,500 km) southeast of New York
Size	13 square miles (21 square km)
	8 miles (12 km) long by 5 miles (8 km) wide
Highest point	High North, 955 feet (299 m)
Population	7,000
Language	English
Time	Atlantic Standard Time (1 hour ahead of EST, same as EDT)
Area code	473
Electricity	220/240 volts AC, 50 cycles
Currency	The Eastern Caribbean dollar, EC$ (EC$2.68 = US$1)
Driving	On the LEFT; a local permit is required and will be provided for $12 with a valid driver's license.
Documents	Valid passport (recommended) or proof of nationality (with photo) and an ongoing or return ticket
Departure tax	$20
Beer to drink	Heineken
Rum to drink	Jack Iron
Music to hear	Dancehall
Tourism info	800-927-9554 or 212-687-9554
	www.grenadagrenadines.com

5:30 p.m. Monday–Friday, and departs the main dock in Hillsborough, Carriacou, for Grenada, at 6 a.m. and 3:30 p.m. Schedules are slightly different (and reduced) on weekends. Fares are about $16 each way ($30 round-trip). Note that when seas are remotely rough, the crossing inspires motion sickness among passengers. For those in search of a slow boat, the mail boat comes up from St. George's daily except Sunday, Monday, and Thursday. They leave from Carriacou daily except Tuesday, Friday, and Saturday. The fare is about $8 one way, and the crossing takes about four hours. Check schedules before you plan on anything (473-440-2279)—times and dates change often and at will. There is also limited boat service between Carriacou and Union on Monday and Thursday—again, confirm with the tourist office in Grenada.

Getting Around

From early morning to sundown, buses (minivans, in reality) criss-cross the island for under $2. The drivers will be more than happy to throw out all the other passengers and charge you $5 to $10 for a "private taxi," although in the name of brotherhood, understanding, and good PR, we don't recommend doing this. Riding with the other passengers is lots of fun, too. For special and nighttime trips you will have to go private. You can also rent a car on Carriacou for about $40 per day. You must provide a credit card and valid driver's license and obtain a temporary Grenada driver's license for $12. Try **Martin Bullen** at 473-443-7204 and **John Gabriel** at 473-443-7454. Remember, driving is on the *left*, which is easy here due to the minimal traffic, but you might feel (as we once did) as though you've entered a parallel universe and mistake the wiper arm for the turn signal. As we stated earlier, the roads were in bad shape when we visited, with promises of improvement soon. But in Caribbean time...

Focus on Carriacou: Walking

The northern and eastern sides of the island are almost entirely un-inhabited and are traversed by an old plantation road. Spectacular views, 18th-century stone ruins, secluded beaches, and solitude will be your reward for braving the tropical sun and heat. Bring along plenty of water, some sandwiches, and pastries from the bakery in Hillsborough. Should you decide to bushwhack, follow the cow paths down the hillside and into the woods, where you may come upon a mysterious cultivated field of wacky weed (marijuana). It is definitely not a good idea to explore further in that particular direction or to accost any mysterious passersby to inquire about local agricultural practices.

Walk 1: Anse La Roche (half to full day)

Take the road north out of Hillsborough to Bogles. At the end of Bogles take the dirt branch to the left, which climbs up past the Caribbee Inn. Continue on this James Taylor country road shaded by manchineel trees (don't touch—the sap is poisonous—and never stand under them when it rains) until you come to a large tree on the right leaning out over the road. Take the cowpath to the left through the woods, past calabash trees to the ruins of an old plantation. In front is a huge sloping pasture that opens out to a magnificent vista with Union Island looming in the distance. This view is so enjoyable you may not want to proceed further, but by all means do. Follow the trail down to the right until you reach a trail marker (when we were there it was a black rock with a shell on top); then take the steep path down the hill and into the woods again until you get to the beach. It is usually deserted, or with only a few people from the Caribbee or from boats. Snorkeling is good along the rocks on the north (far) end, but save some energy for the hot climb back up.

Walk 2: Windward (half to full day)

Follow the Walk 1 instructions past the Caribbee Inn and past the cutoff to Anse La Roche. Continue on the same plantation road around High North to Gun Point and then to Petit Carenage Bay, where there is a nice deserted beach and a reef for snorkeling. At the right end of the beach is a mangrove swamp called the Bird Swamp. Directly across the bay is Petit St. Vincent, the *trôp chic et cher* resort on its own island, and on the right, Petite Martinique, often just called PM. Try to imagine an international frontier crossing between these two islands—to the north you're in the country called St. Vincent and the Grenadines, whereas everything from Petite Martinique south is part of Grenada. Islanders routinely cross this border without a thought! As you continue on your walk, the road leads into Windward. This is still a major boat-building center. Brightly colored wooden boats can be seen everywhere in the Grenadines, and they are particularly photogenic here on the beach, under construction or repair. As mentioned earlier, most of the residents of Windward are of mixed Scottish and West Indian descent—the Scots came here to build a merchant fleet when Britain ruled the islands.

There are several rum shops and minimarkets to get some refreshment (it can be very hot and dry in Windward). You can hire a boat here to take you to PM or to sail up the Grenadines to the Tobago Cays or Canouan. We had a very good experience sailing with Zev MacLaren on his hand-built boat, the *Sweetheart*. You can get back to Hillsborough by continuing to follow the road around across the island to Bogles.

Walk 3: Grand Bay–Kendeace Point–Sabazan–Six Roads (full day)

This is a serious walk for the more dedicated hiker, but it is well worth the effort. Take a bus or taxi over to Grand Bay—it is too steep and too far to walk. At the bus stop, walk down to the right until you discover the old plantation road that leads south and then west. You will reach Kendeace Point fairly quickly, but don't bother to bushwhack out onto the point. Instead, follow the cow patty trail down to the spectacular and totally deserted beach just to the north of the point. As you follow the road around to Sabazan, you won't see a single sign of human habitation, except some old stone ruins. Up on the hill at Sabazan, you'll see some fairly spectacular ruins peeking above the treeline. Getting to them is not as easy as it looks, and it is recommended only for the determined archaeologist or historian. At Sabazan Bay there is a beautiful beach, with a lovely little cove for swimming on the north side and some weirdly wonderful wind-sculpted trees on the south end. At Dumfries make sure you take the cutoff up to the right, past the lime factory ruins, to Six Roads, or you'll be in for a very long hike indeed. There is a rum shop at Six Roads for refreshment, and at that point you'll be glad to know it is only a short and easy walk back into Hillsborough.

Where to Stay

Contrary to most Caribbean islands, there has been little growth in the range of accommodations offered on Carriacou. There are only around 100 beds available on the island. The nicest place to stay is still the Caribbee Inn. On our last visit, Cassada Bay was still having management and financial issues — we'd love for some enterprising individual to take over this spectacular spot and give it a fresh coat of paint.

⊛ **The Caribbee Inn,** Prospect, Carriacou, Grenada, W.I. ℂ 473-443-7380, ✆ 473-443-8142, 🖳 www.caribbeeinn.com, caribbeeinn@caribsurf.com

💰 **Not So Cheap** for rooms, **Pricey** for suites 🍴 **EP** (closed during September and/or October, depending on the whims of the Coopers)

In its former incarnation as the Prospect Lodge, this was everyone's ideal of a Caribbean inn; it was run by the legendary Lee and Ann Katzenbach, artists and hippies who provided a truly stimulating atmosphere for dirt-cheap prices. Under the stewardship of the current owners, Brits Robert and Wendy Cooper, prices have increased, but who could blame them? No one could figure out how Lee and Ann were doing it. The Coopers have also lent a distinctly British air to the Caribbee, have added three suites, and are now morphing the inn into a nature-oriented resort.

The Caribbee still has the best location on Carriacou, perched high over the ocean, in the woods on the island's northern coast. Set on 12 acres, it borders High North, a 1,000-acre wooded National Park — hence the focus on nature. It's a five-minute jaunt down the hill to a small rocky beach. In addition, it's a 20-minute walk to Anse La Roche (Carriacou's prettiest beach). To town, it's a longish, though manageable, walk into Hillsborough. The compound includes two rooms in the main building, two in an adjacent building, and three suites in a newer building. The four original rooms have ceramic-tile floors, wooden-jalousied windows held open by poles, four-poster beds, mosquito netting, minibars and minifridges, tea-making facilities (jolly good!), small libraries, and hammocks. None of these rooms has hot water, but all have names. Our favorite is the Planter's Suite. The three suites do have solar hot water and are much larger. The grandest of the three is called Sparrow Bay, with high ceilings and velvet drapes. The lower unit, Colonial, was used by Conde Nast Traveler for a *Room with a View* shot—yes, it's that scenic.

The Caribbee's common areas are warm and bright, with a touch of antiques here and there and a cute little bar. The Coopers—who somehow remind us of pioneers from the days when the sun never set on the Empire—inject their own brand of English charm and raise a flock of clamorous macaws at their adjoining home. Wendy Cooper is a Cordon Bleu chef and has created an excellent French Creole menu that emphasizes seafood and local produce and spices. Robert is a former actor and theater manager and is said to arrange impromptu readings of Shakespeare when fellow actors visit. They blithely and apologetically promote Caribbee as Carriacou's only repository of civilization. That's not much of an overstatement, but on this eccentric island, the Coopers also seem to fit in quite nicely.

Bogles Round House Cottages, Bogles, Carriacou, Grenada, W.I.
　Ⓒ 473-443-7841, 🖂 same as phone, 🖥 www.grenadines.net/
carriacou/russell.htm, roundhouse@grenadines.net
🔸 Cheap 🍽 EP Ⓒ🅒

Opened as a restaurant and bar by former New York chef Kate Stroebel, the Round House also has three cute gingerbread-style efficiency cottages with fully equipped galley kitchens, private baths, ceiling fans, bedside tables, reading lamps, mosquito netting, and lanais. Well maintained and private, the inn is only 100 feet away from the beach. There is twice-weekly maid service. The Round House Restaurant & Bar has been the island's best and serves breakfast and dinner for guests. However, at press time, the Roundhouse was under new management, as Kate was leaving to open a new restaurant in Hillsborough called The Garden (Fall 2003).

Silver Beach Cottages, Silver Beach, Beausejour Bay, Carriacou, Grenada, W.I. ℂ Stateside: 800-742-4276, Local: 473-443-7337, ✆ 473-443-7165, 🖳 silverbeach@caribsurf.com

🛍 Cheap 🍴 EP ⒸⒸ

This is a 16-room, West Indian–owned and –run hotel on the northern edge of Hillsborough. It is on the water, but since it is adjacent to the town wharf, it's not a great place for swimming. The rooms are comfortable and modern, with ceiling fans, private baths, and lanais. There are semidetached efficiency units out back. The food in the Shipwreck Restaurant is good, and the bar is the place to meet locals.

Green Roof Inn, Bogles, Carriacou, Grenada, W.I. ℂ 473-443-6399, ✆ same as phone, 🖳 www.greenroofinn.com, greenroof@caribsurf.com

🛍 Cheap 🍴 CP ⒸⒸ

Set on a hill overlooking Hillsborough Bay, the Green Roof Inn is a newer six-room, two-story guest house owned by a Swedish couple, Janas and Asa. Rooms are very simple but clean. Four have private baths. There is a spacious restaurant and bar overlooking the bay—a great place for a sunset cocktail. Bicycles are available free of charge to guests.

Where to Eat

Basically, you eat at your hotel on Carriacou—especially dinner. Or try these:

$$ **Callaloo by the Sea**, Hillsborough, 473-443-8004
Serving West Indian fare from 10 a.m. to 10 p.m. daily in season, this pleasant spot sits on the water and has great callaloo soup as well as dependable Creole chicken and curried conch.

$$$$ **The Caribbee Inn**, Prospect, 473-443-7380
Excellent French Creole cuisine emphasizing seafood and local produce and spices by Cordon Bleu chef Wendy Cooper is

served in a warm and appealing candlelit setting. Reservations a must.

$$$ **The Garden,** Hillsborough, (phone not available at press time) Kate Stroebel has left the Roundhouse to open her own restaurant in town. None of the particulars are known at press time, except that Kate ran the best restaurant on the island and will probably maintain her reputation with The Garden. The menu should feature fresh fish, pastas, and salads.

$$$ **Green Roof Inn,** Bogles, 473-443-6399
This Swedish-run restaurant serves European-style preparations of fish, lobster gratinée, and filet mignon. The sunset view is smashing from the open-air terrace.

$$$ **The Round House Restaurant & Bar,** Bogles, 473-443-7841
The Round House is indeed in a curvy, round building made of stone; it features a tree in the center. Under new management and a new chef, we hope that the restaurant will maintain its superb reputation. Open for breakfast and dinner daily for guests, and dinner only (with reservations) for nonguests.

Don't Miss

Sandy Cay

About a half-mile offshore, this tiny island of creamy sand and palm trees offers a beautiful spot for a day's outing. There is also a fantastic reef for snorkeling off the northern end of the cay, with huge coral heads and a large variety of fish. Your hotel can arrange for a boat to get you there. Unfortunately, the odds are you won't be alone on the beach. This is a regular pit stop for the yacht and cruise contingents.

Canute Caliste

The most famous artist in the lower Caribbean, Mr. Caliste paints, in the primitive style, such traditional Kayak subjects as Big Drum, the Quadrille, Carnival, boat-building, and fishing—and also such supernatural characters as mermaids and jagluars (Carriacou's version of the vampire). Caliste's work has been displayed at the White House and Buckingham Palace, and the British publishing firm Macmillan has published a book of his paintings. A few pieces are displayed in the Carriacou Museum (where he sometimes hangs out), located across from the tourist office in town. He was born in 1914, and his daughter told us that he no longer paints (his paintings in the last few years have little vitality). Sadder still is that sloppy "storage" at the museum allowed a number of his works to be damaged by a storm in 2002. You might also want to visit another island painter, **Frankie Francis**, who lives in L'Esterre and works in Hillsborough at the telephone company. In his thirties, he is as handsome as a movie star and paints charming island scenes.

⊛ **Carnival**

Either because people got too rowdy for the tourists or because there was too much competition from Carnival in Trinidad, Carnival on Grenada was moved to August. However, on Carriacou it still takes place during the traditional week before Ash Wednesday. Here it is a lovely and charming small-town celebration with an intricate structure rooted in tradition. Each town spends the weeks leading up to Carnival making elaborate costumes for their queen (a young woman chosen for looks, talent, and style) and her court, called a band. Each queen and her band illustrate a theme, such as "the solar system" or "back to nature." On the Saturday a week and a half before Ash Wednesday, the festivities kick off with a parodistic competition—the choosing of a male "queen" and a female "king." The real competition occurs a week later when the genuine Carnival queen and her band of the year are chosen. Other features include a "dirty *mas*," when everybody gets totally tanked and smears everybody else (including you—dress accordingly!) with mud and ashes; a "clean *mas*," when everyone parades around in their Sunday best; a calypso contest; a parade on Shrove Tuesday; and an extraordinary custom peculiar to Carriacou—the "fighting *mas*," in which the men dress up as Pierrots and wander around reciting Shakespeare and beating each other with sticks (we're not kidding). If the thought of Carnival in Brazil or Trinidad intimidates, this is the one for you. The people are warm and welcoming, and should you get tired of celebrating, just get out of Hillsborough.

Big Drum

Another custom unique to Carriacou is Big Drum, also known as "nation dances." It is an all-night celebration featuring percussive music that stems from African tribal drumming. There are three drums made of rum kegs and goatskins, and the music is accompanied by a highly intricate and beautiful dance. Big Drum is played at most important island occasions — boat launchings, house blessings, and tombstone dedications, among them. You will be fortunate indeed to be invited.

Regatta

Featuring boat races and even more onshore fun, Regatta is the big hoo-ha of the Grenadines. The racing is really secondary to the drinking and other shenanigans characteristic of all Caribbean sailing regattas. It lasts four days (around the first week of August) and features such frolicking summer-camp activities as greased-pole, tug-of-war, and donkey races. For more information, contact the Grenada Board of Tourism.

Diving

The clear, calm waters around Carriacou provide some excellent dive sites. Call **Carriacou Silver Diving** (473-443-7882), a family-run shop that does everything from Discover Scuba courses through Instructor Training, or **Tanki's** (473-443-8406).

Mustique

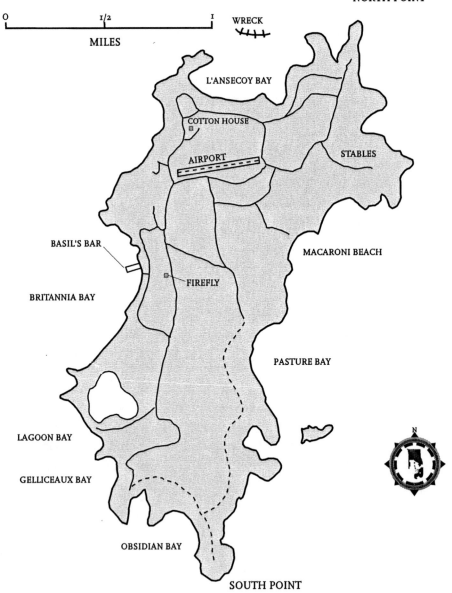

NORTH POINT

0   1/2   1

MILES

WRECK

L'ANSECOY BAY

COTTON HOUSE

AIRPORT

STABLES

BASIL'S BAR

MACARONI BEACH

FIREFLY

BRITANNIA BAY

PASTURE BAY

LAGOON BAY

N

GELLICEAUX BAY

OBSIDIAN BAY

SOUTH POINT

Mustique

"DAH-LING, IT'S FABOO!" THOSE ARE THE WORDS WE overheard about a gorgeous waterfront and pool-adorned stucco mansion, seen as we were landing at Mustique airport's tiny, sloping runway. We later learned it was for sale for millions and millions (way beyond our budget). This made us recall our impression of Mustique on our first visit to this small, private island of the rich and famous in 1987. Arriving by boat (we weren't as well off in those days), we were overwhelmed by the vision of the huge Italianate mansion of Harding Lawrence and ad queen Mary Wells. It still sits on a hilltop like the House of Zeus on Mount Olympus, although the plantings surrounding it have matured and now partly shield it from view. Apparently things haven't changed much here, except that there are a lot more villas on the island and construction seems to be going on everywhere. The late H.R.H. Princess Margaret and her son, Viscount Linley, used to come here every year to her villa, called Les Jolies Eaux (it has since been sold). Schmatta-king Tommy Hilfiger has built a very large, over-the-top mansion that screams "Look at me!" on L'Ansecoy Beach. Down the road is Mick Jagger's Japanese-style beach house called Stargroves, a lesson in good taste — private, secluded, and unobtrusive (and can be rented for $16,000/week). Speaking of rock stars, David Bowie and Elton John once owned villas here, too. Welcome to Mustique, vacationland of the rich, famous, and even more rich.

Owned by the Mustique Company, Ltd., this is the Caribbean's small, private Martha's Vineyard without the New England quaintness and restraint. Many of the opulent villas resemble separate miniresorts in the Victorian gingerbread mold, elevated to the appropriate grandness. Besides the Cotton House and the Firefly Guest House, there are only about 75 houses on the island. A glance

Mustique: Key Facts

Location	13°N by 61°W
	18 miles (30 km) south of St. Vincent
	110 miles (177 km) west of Barbados
	2,060 miles (3,315 km) southeast of New York
Size	2 square miles (5.2 square km)
Highest point	Fort Shandy, 496 feet (151 m)
Population	About 600
Language	English
Time	Atlantic Standard Time (1 hour ahead of EST, same as EDT)
Area code	784
Electricity	220 volts AC, 50 cycles
Currency	The Eastern Caribbean dollar, EC$ (EC$2.68 = US$1)
Driving	On the LEFT; U.S. and Canadian citizens must present a valid driver's license and pay $28 to obtain a temporary local driver's permit.
Documents	Canadian and U.S. citizens must have proof of citizenship with photo ID (we recommend a valid passport), plus an on-going or return ticket.
Departure tax	$13
Beer to drink	Hairoun
Rum to drink	Any Vincentian brand
Music to hear	The Stones
Tourism info	800-225-4255 or 203-602-0300
	www.mustique-island.com

at the property titles would reveal a global representation of the fabulous and fortunate. No cruise ships here, as they and boats with more than 25 passengers are prohibited from visiting.

Don't know somebody with a villa? Well, you can easily rent one from the Mustique Company. At last count, there are 55 available, at weekly prices from $6,500 (or $3,500 in low season) for a two-bedroom without pool to $27,000 for a spectacular nine-bedroom, Japanese-styled affair that wraps around a koi pond. Or you can stay at the Cotton House on the northwest corner of the island. It's discreetly tasteful, with 20 rooms tucked into two plantation houses and three whitewashed, almost Swedish-looking cottages. All details are looked after, as is to be expected. The pool is small, but who swims, anyway? The main activity here is to have a drink, maybe a bite to eat, sit by the pool, and see who shows up. Visually, the pool ensemble is stunning. London stage, set, and costume designer Oliver Messel framed it with the remnants of an old sugar mill warehouse, its jagged edge outlined against the sky, while the pool itself conjures up memories of the Clampetts' pool in *The Beverly Hillbillies*. Looking north from the pool, you can see the tennis courts and rooftops of a famous rock legend's compound giving him shelter. The beach in that direction, L'Ansecoy Bay, is very pretty and looks out on the wreck of the Antilles, a French cruise ship that ran a reef in 1971.

It used to be that if the Cotton House didn't fit your style or budget, there was an alternative: the Firefly Guest House. Its old motto was "You don't have to be rich and famous to enjoy Mustique." That's not the case anymore. Since being acquired and reinvented by Brits Stan and Elizabeth Clayton, it's now "Not an hotel—an experience." Right. We think that "You don't have to be famous, but you do have to be rich to enjoy Mustique" is more appropriate, as rates have skyrocketed (so much for the penny-pinching masses!). The Firefly's cozy bar and restaurant is where the island's branché residents and guests hang out when the sun sets (if they go out at all).

The hub of activity for Mustique's tourists is most certainly Basil's Beach Bar. Located on Britannia Bay along with Basil's Market, Boutique, and Water Sports Center, it's a favorite with both the yachting set and occasional celebutantes. His thatched-roof beach-bar-on-stilts also serves lunch and dinner, featuring fresh lobster as well as beef, chicken, and veggie dishes. On Wednesday nights during the winter season, there is a barbecue and jump-up with pan bands from Bequia or St. Vincent. It's very possible you'll recognize someone—the tip-off is the bodyguard(s). Basil's T-shirts are great collector's items and can be bought at Basil's Boutique. Neighboring Johanna Morris's Treasure Boutiques, set in two vividly colored gingerbread-style houses, also has souvenirs available. Tucked between the two houses is Johanna Banana, featuring Italian espresso, ice cream, breakfast, homemade pastries, and fresh fruit juices.

The Briefest History

Mustique was once inhabited by the Arawaks, then the Caribs, who were wiped out by England in the 18th century. In the 1700s, the island was used for sugarcane, and was heavily guarded against the French (hence the remains of three forts still visible today). With the advent of the sugar beet and declining sugar prices, the island dwindled, with 100-or-so fishermen and farmers living in a neglected settlement called Cheltenham. They eeked out a meager existence that had little to do with the glimmering beaches curling around the island's perimeter. In 1958 Scotsman Colin Tennant (né Lord Glenconner) bought Mustique from the Hazell family. The purchase price: reportedly about $100,000! Tennant had a master stroke when he gifted England's Princess Margaret with a 10-acre (4.5 hectare) plot as a wedding present in 1960. The fanciful gift helped to put the island on the map as a potential playground for celebrities and royalty. Within a few years, Tennant built a new village for the islanders, and in 1968 he started the Mustique Company with the St. Vincent government to develop 140 high-end homes. An airstrip was built, and in 1969 famed British theatrical designer Oliver Messel helped to create Cotton House (on the grounds of the former Cheltenham) and the initial villas.

Getting There

Somehow Mustique's developers squeezed a runway onto the island. Since there are no landing lights, it can receive small planes, and only until dusk. The easiest way to get here is via Barbados and connecting to **Mustique Airways** or **SVG Air**. Both also provide scheduled flights from St. Vincent, St. Lucia, Grenada, and Martinique. If you are on Bequia or another Grenadine, you can hire a boat to take you over for a day trip. From Bequia, it will cost around $200 (depending on your negotiating skills) for the round-trip hire of boat and crew. It makes sense to fill the boat with a group (usually up to 10), since the cost is the same for 1 or 10. This is a great way to see the island if you are staying on Bequia.

Focus on Mustique: Exploring the Island

The island is small, comprising only 1,400 acres (about 560 hectares). It can be seen fairly easily by renting a jeep, motorcycle, or a Mule (not an animal, it's a Kawasaki that resembles a rugged, souped-up golf cart). We rented a Mule for $60 per day. You can also hire a taxi for about $40 an hour, and an hour is sufficient for a cursory visit of the island. Starting the tour at the Cotton House, pick up a map at the office and have a drink by the pool. After a few refreshments, stop by the boutique in the windmill (it's cute, and they now have Cotton House T-shirts). Hop in your Mule or vehicle (the driver, of course, being sober) and proceed north to L'Ansecoy Beach. Here you'll pass Messrs. Jagger's and Hilfiger's villas, and while we can't tell you exactly where they are (our lawyer's advice), most astute readers will figure it out (or just ask a local). After passing the eastern end of the airport runway, turn right and pass the stables and tennis courts. At the second intersection, go straight up the hill and then screaming down a steep winding descent to the waterfront and Basil's. Time out for more refreshments.

When ready, follow the road along Britannia Bay until just past the jetty, and jog to the left. At the end, take a right, and within a short distance you'll be at the Firefly. Be sure to stop in and check it out (the bar opens around 4 p.m. and it's definitely a place to be seen). Continue on your drive and stay to the right at the fork, then go straight until you come to another intersection with a fork. The left fork goes uphill and the right one goes down. First go right. This will lead you to sheltered Lagoon Bay, which offers swimming possibilities for those of you who want to cool off. Returning to the fork, take a sharp right up the hill. This will take you past Gelliceaux Bay (the island's best snorkeling is found on the bay's northern end –and also on Lagoon Bay's southern end) and the late Princess Maggie's place. At the next major fork, bear left again or you'll end up in

Obsidian Bay. The road here is rough in spots and mostly unpaved. Keep going until you see signs for Pasture Bay, Mustique's prettiest beach — but off-limits to swimming due to a fierce undertow.

Enjoy the scenery and at the first fork, bear right. This will take you north until a sharp right and signs for Macaroni Beach — the island's most popular and the best for swimming. It's a curving beach of white sand and palm trees, with a few thatched-roof huts for shade. Time out for a swim. When you're ready, head back the same way and go to the end of the road, turn left, and then go right at the next intersection. The runway will be in front of you. A quick left and right will return you to the Cotton House. Time out for a swim in Endeavour Bay (good snorkeling on the northern side of the dock) and a cocktail (drivers included). You know where to go.

Where to Stay

If you really want to *do* Mustique with panache — and it's the best way to stay here if you are with a group or family — you can rent one of about 55 villas of various sizes, degrees of luxury, and location. Prices start at $3,500 per week (low season) and $6,500 (high season) for a two-bedroom villa that sleeps four, without a pool. The late Princess Margaret's five-bedroom villa, Les Jolies Eaux, goes for $18,000 in winter (references required, of course). Rates include airport transfers, household staff of at least three, vehicle rental, laundry service and access to floodlit tennis courts. Contact the **Mustique Company**, P.O. Box 349, Mustique, St. Vincent and The Grenadines, W.I. Local: 784-458-4621, fax 784-456-4565, or if you want to save up for the villa, call 800-225-4255.

Or you can stay at the following.

⊛ **The Cotton House**, P.O. Box 349, Mustique, St. Vincent and the Grenadines, W.I. ℂ Stateside: 800-223-1108, Local: 784-456-4777, ✆ 784-456-5887, ▢ www.cottonhouse.net, info@cottonhouse.net

💲 **Stratospheric** ⑪ **BP** (a MAP rate is also available). The hotel is closed late August to late October.

Situated on a private beach by Endeavour Bay, the Cotton House is the destination resort of celebrities and royalty. If you don't happen to be a celebrity or of real royal lineage, don't worry—you will be treated as if you are. Twenty guest cottages, suites, and rooms make up this luxury hotel. Each has either a king-size bed or twin beds, air conditioning, ceiling fans, minibar, mosquito netting, telephone, and CD player with a CD menu (we love that touch, but bring your own music— the menu was geared toward a senior market). They also come with a valet who will unpack your bags and press your clothes upon arrival (we love this, too!). We found some nice little touches that set the Cotton House apart from the rest—a bottle of rosewater spray to cool your face (one upon arrival and another when departing at the airport), Egyptian cotton linens and towels, and a personal pillow menu. We went gaga over the pillows and chose down ones of different firmnesses (you can even reserve one ahead of your arrival).

The Great House is spacious and airy. There is a bar inside, and lots of comfy chairs and couches for sitting, relaxing, having a drink, or reading a book—either in the main room or on the veranda. It also boasts a fabulous restaurant that serves breakfast, lunch, and dinner. The cuisine is a good mix of Caribbean and French, and the wine list is superb. We found the staff very accommodating. Room service is available. A variety of activities can be arranged, including tennis, horseback riding, water sports, massage, and island trips. Upon your arrival, make sure you take advantage of the island tour they offer, conducted by the hotel's chauffeur, Bobsin.

Firefly Guest House, P.O. Box 349, Mustique, St. Vincent and the Grendadines, W.I. © 784-456-3414, ✆ 784-456-3514, 🖥 www.mustiquefirefly.com, stan@mustiquefirefly.com

💰 **Stratospheric** 🍴 **FAP** CC

Stan and Elizabeth Clayton have certainly changed things since first taking over the Firefly in 1995. All four rooms have been completely redone and are redecorated every six months.

Even though the rooms are on the small side, they are very luxurious — from the four-poster king- or queen-size bed with Egyptian cotton linens, to the unbleached cotton towels, to the magnificent view of Britannia Bay. All rooms have ceiling or regular fans (two have air conditioning), minibar, telephone, and room service. Perched on a steep hillside, the Firefly has two freshwater swimming pools (connected by a rock water-fall and surrounded by lush tropical gardens), sundecks, private patios, a barbecue, and a garden bar.

The Firefly's bar and restaurant is the hot spot on the island, where the in crowd goes and where those in the know hang out. This is where you will see celebs as well as local homeowners and hotel guests eating dinner on the terrace or chatting over a Mustique Cocktail in the lounge area. There is a grand piano where a pianist provides entertainment every night from December to February. We particularly like the Mustique Martini Club. Drink all 14 and get a free Martini Club polo shirt (now *that* is a collector's item!). Or there's the Mustique Champagne Club. Drink all eight champagne cocktails and earn a Champagne Club polo.

The restaurant serves breakfast, lunch, picnics, and dinners, all prepared by chef Keith Taylor, who creates a fusion cuisine of international and Caribbean fare. After the candlelit dinner on the terrace, the lounge area heats up with the atmosphere of someone's living room rather than a bar. The Claytons do their best to make you feel at home (a very nice home, indeed, we might add!). They even throw in a Mule (that's a vehicle, not an animal) with the rates, so all in all it's still cheaper than Cotton House — but don't come to Mustique if you're even remotely thinking of watching your wallet. Hell, this place even has its own line of designer sarongs!

Where to Eat

There are now four choices: Your rented villa (have the cook whip up something light for you tonight), or any of the following three choices. Be sure to make reservations wherever you choose to dine.

$$$$$ ⊛ The Cotton House, Cotton House, 784-456-4777
Dining on the Great House veranda is a very extraordinary experience indeed. We were impressed with the food, the service, the wine list, and the prices (but, then, this *is* Mustique, so who cares?). The cuisine is a French-Caribbean fusion by Chef Emmanuel Guemon. Open daily for breakfast, lunch, and dinner.

$$$$$ ⊛ Firefly, Firefly Guest House, 784-456-3414
The other great (and celeb-heavy) restaurant on Mustique is the Firefly. Chef Keith Taylor prepares his fusion cuisine of international and Caribbean fare. Dinner is served on the candlelit terrace. The restaurant is open for breakfast, lunch, and dinner.

$$$$ Basil's Bar, Brittania Bay, 784-456-3350
Basil's is probably Mustique's biggest tourist attraction (besides celebrity-spotting), but since Mustique doesn't really have any tourists beside island guests and the occasional yacht, this "beach bar" on a pier is an institution on Mustique, as is Basil. Given its location, the emphasis is on fresh seafood. Speaking of yachties, Basil's is a favorite watering hole and is Mustique's "nightclub." Open daily for lunch, dinner, and, of course, sunset cocktails.

Don't Miss

Drinks at Basil's and the Firefly

The island's two happening bars are both worth a visit after dinner. Basil's especially hops on Wednesdays during the winter season, and it's anyone's guess who'll show up at the Firefly on a given night.

⊛ Mustique Blues Festival

First held in 1996, this brainchild of Basil Charles and Dana Gillespie is now an annual event and the Caribbean's only blues festival. Held at Basil's Bar, usually at the end of January through early February, proceeds benefit the Basil

Charles Educational Foundation. The Foundation provides scholarships for the children of St. Vincent. For more information, visit www.basilsmustique.com/blues.htm.

The Smaller Grenadines

Canouan

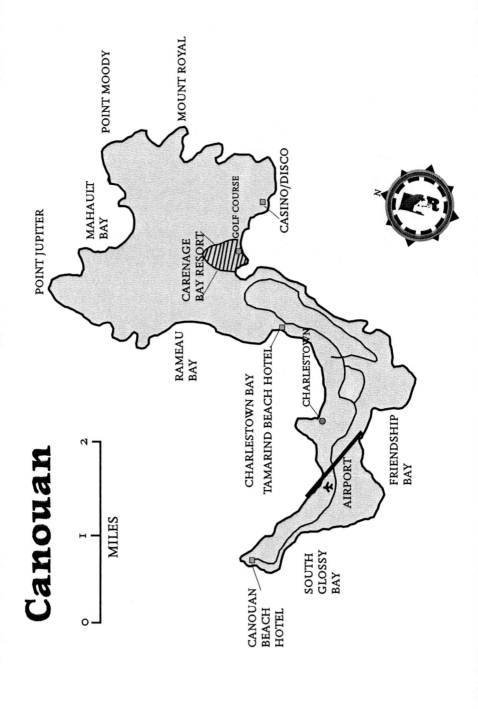

MILES

0   1   2

N

POINT JUPITER

POINT MOODY

MOUNT ROYAL

MAHAULT BAY

RAMEAU BAY

GOLF COURSE

CARENAGE BAY RESORT

CASINO/DISCO

CHARLESTOWN BAY

TAMARIND BEACH HOTEL

CHARLESTOWN

AIRPORT

FRIENDSHIP BAY

SOUTH GLOSSY BAY

CANOUAN BEACH HOTEL

Canouan

WHEN WE FIRST STARTED TOOLING AROUND THE CARIB-
bean, five-square-mile Canouan was one of the more remote and
undeveloped corners of the region. Not anymore. Over the last few
years, the 800-acre Carenage Bay Beach Resort has been built, with
a lavish casino, stunning golf course and swank villas. Can you say
"Mustique, Part Deux?" Although there have been a few hiccups along
the way to glory, we predict that in a few years Canouan will be on a
par with its famed neighbor as a premier landing for the famous and
moneyed.

The island is physically beautiful, with a half-dozen fine beaches,
a stunning, three-mile-long reef protecting the east coast, and a tidy
little village, built courtesy of the rising standard of living brought by
the arrival of a $200 million resort.

Getting There

Believe it or not, Canouan's airport is the most advanced in the country, equipped for night landings and larger planes (though not jets),
unlike the one on St. Vincent. At this writing, a heavily subsidized
(thank you, Carenage management) **American Eagle** flight arrives
several days a week en route to and from Barbados and San Juan. On
our most recent visit, only three passengers boarded the flight to San
Juan, two of whom were **American Eagle** employees! You can also
reach Canouan on **TIA** from Barbados, on **Mustique Airways** from
Barbados and St. Vincent, and **SVG Air** from Grenada and St. Vincent.

Getting Around

Since the island is so small (only three miles long by one mile wide),
a rental car really isn't necessary. All hotels will meet you at the

airport. The Carenage Bay Resort and the Tamarind Beach Hotel provide a shuttle service between these two facilities. The Canouan Beach
Hotel is at the extreme southern end of the island and is within walking distance of the airport terminal. Cars are available, however, for
about $60 per day and can be arranged through your hotel.

Where to Stay

⊛ **Carenage Bay Beach and Golf Club,** Canouan, St. Vincent and
   the Grenadines, W.I. ℭ Stateside: 888-767-3966, Local:
   784-458-8000, ✉ 784-458-8885, ⌨ www.canouan.com,
   info@canouan.com

   💲 **Stratospheric** (but watch for specials when the hotel
   reopens in late 2003) 🍴 **EP** ©©

   Construction of the Carenage Bay Resort forever changed the
   face of sleepy Canouan. Although we frown on the development of a once unspoiled place, Carenage Bay is a monumen-
   tal achievement. Built by a consortium of Italian investors
   and a Swiss bank, the project encompasses two-thirds of the
   1,900-acre island. About half of the property is devoted to a
   155-room resort and golf course (which opened in late 1999),
   and the remainder will be sold off to investors for holiday
   homes (à la Mustique). The first half-dozen of these homes
   had been completed when we last visited, in early 2003, and
   they are pretty special. Our site inspection took place at
   an unusual point, however, because the hotel was midway
   through a projected one-and-a-half-year-long closure. The
   Carenage owners had hired Rosewood Hotels & Resorts (of
   Caneel Bay and Little Dix fame) to run Carenage, but in early
   2002, Rosewood's management contract was terminated (the
   two outfits are currently in litigation). The hotel was closed
   for major refurbishing (after just three years!), during which
   a few design problems are being ironed out, in particular the
   ill-conceived golf course. A new management company for
   Carenage and its anticipated late 2003 reopening had not

been announced as of press time (and it's anybody's guess when it will reopen).

Set on the site of an old village (the church is still standing and has been restored), the resort made us gasp the first time we saw it from above. Located in a valley on the east coast, it has more than 100 colorfully painted villas and buildings designed by the late Italian architect Luigi Vietti scattered about the resort. Other highlights include the Grenadines' largest pool (one of the largest in all the Caribbean) and Jacuzzi, three lighted tennis courts, a health and fitness center, a full-service spa, the Trump-managed casino, the Blue Moon Nightclub, four restaurants, several bars, and all kinds of water sports, including scuba. A major focus is the 18-hole golf course, redesigned by Jim Fazio. When it reopens it is almost sure to rival the esteemed Four Seasons Nevis course for spectacular vistas and challenging play. There are two main beaches fronting the resort (these are terrific), and at least two more found in an (as yet) undeveloped part of the property.

The rooms are remarkably tasteful and well appointed. Amenities include lanais, air conditioning, ceiling fans, safes, minibars and minifridges, bathrobes, twice-daily housekeeping, phones with data ports, and satellite TV. Some suites also have kitchenettes. The decor is a Tuscan-Sardinian fusion, with earth-toned walls and fabrics, natural woods, and terra-cotta tiles. Beds have Frette cotton sheets and feather pillows. The baths feature strikingly colorful glazed tiles, hand-painted sinks, large vanities (we love that), showers, and the requisite big tubs and bidets (for Europeans, that is). Laundry, dry cleaning, in-room catering, and baby-sitting services are available, too.

Tamarind Beach Hotel & Yacht Club, Charlestown, Canouan, St. Vincent and the Grenadines, W.I. ℰ 784-458-8044, ℰ 784-458-8851, ⌨ www.tamarindbeachhotel.com, cantbh@caribsurf.com

💼 Very Pricey and up **🍴 EP** CC

Spruced up during the Carenage closure (and owned by the same folks), the Tamarind sits on a pretty beach facing west and is at the edge of Charlestown, Canouan's only village. Strung along the beach in four two-story blue-roof buildings, there are 43 rooms, all with lanais, wood walls, wicker furnishings, tiled floors, ceiling fans (no air conditioning), bright fabrics, minibar, safe, good-size bathrooms and twice-daily maid service. The Palapa Restaurant features surprisingly good Italian and Creole cuisine, and the Pirate Cove bar is a great place for a snack and sunset cocktails. All kinds of water sports are available or can be arranged by the hotel. The Moorings charter sail operation has established a Grenadines base here.

Canouan Beach Hotel, P.O. Box 530, South Glossy Bay, Canouan, St. Vincent and the Grenadines, W.I. ✆ 784-458-8888, 🖂 784-458-8875, 🖵 www.grenadines.net/canouan/canouanbeachhotelhomepage.htm, cbh@grenadines.net

💼 Wicked Pricey 🍴 All-inclusive CC

Located at the western end of Canouan's tiny new airport and within walking distance of the terminal, this is Canouan's original hotel, owned by and catering to the French. There are 35 rooms situated in bungalows on the beach, with air conditioning, tiled floors, white walls, simple furnishings, lanais, and private baths. Operated as a low-scale all-inclusive resort, the rates include meals, most beverages (French wine with dinner, and an evening rum punch), and limited water sports and day sails. The restaurant here serves French Creole cuisine and is quite good. The price is decent for what you get, but you need to be comfortable with a mostly Euro crowd, and we noted a major mosquito problem during our last visit (the latter could be seasonal).

Where to Eat

The resorts rule the dining scene on Canouan, which is basically a one-company island these days.

$$$–
$$$$$ **Carenage Bay Beach and Golf Club**, 784-458-8000
　　　At press time, the Carenage Bay resort, with its many restaurants, was closed for renovations. When it reopens in late 2003, there should be at least five dining options on site. In addition, there will be a nightclub to shake your groove thang.

$$$$　⊛**Palapa Restaurant**, Tamarind Beach Hotel, 784-458-8044
　　　This is a good place to dine al fresco and overlooking the water. More informal than Carenage (but with reciprocity — guests can charge their meals to Carenage and vice versa), we like the mix of sailors and resort guests. It makes the atmosphere more interesting.

$$　　**Pirate's Cove**, Tamarind Beach Hotel, 784-458-8044
　　　Basically, this is a casual snack-bar where bathing suits are de rigeur.

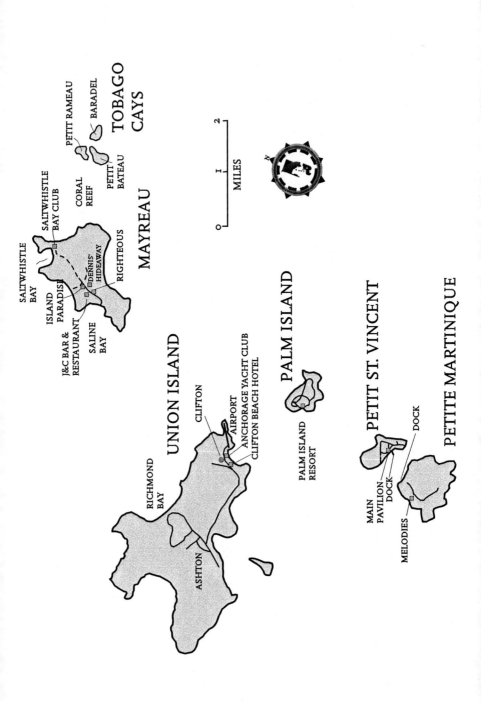

TOBAGO CAYS

PETIT RAMEAU

BARADEL

PETIT BATEAU

MAYREAU

CORAL REEF

SALTWHISTLE BAY CLUB

SALTWHISTLE BAY

ISLAND PARADISE

DENNIS' HIDEAWAY

RIGHTEOUS

J&C BAR & RESTAURANT

SALINE BAY

UNION ISLAND

CLIFTON

AIRPORT

ANCHORAGE YACHT CLUB

CLIFTON BEACH HOTEL

RICHMOND BAY

ASHTON

PALM ISLAND

PALM ISLAND RESORT

PETIT ST. VINCENT

DOCK

MAIN PAVILION

DOCK

MELODIES

PETITE MARTINIQUE

MILES

0   1   2

N

Mayreau

TOURISTO SCALE

TALK ABOUT GETTING AWAY FROM IT ALL. NO ELECTRICITY. No phones. No cars. Hell, there are no roads. Well, we exaggerate. After all, this is the third millennium. The government installed a tiny power station on the island in 2002, so electricity no longer comes from a half-dozen generators that putter through the night. The local establishments have phones, and there are two phone booths on the island where you can access an overseas operator for credit card calls (yes, contact with the outside world is possible). Until recently donkeys were used to carry supplies from the bay up to the village. Now there are three cars, which ferry goods to and from the twice-weekly ferry from St. Vincent. There is also one concrete road that leads from Saline Bay — the port — up the hill to the village and down the hill on the other side to Saltwhistle Bay, one of the most picture-perfect beaches in all the Caribbean.

Still, despite all the "progress," Mayreau is a step back in time — peaceful, relaxed, and a perfect getaway from the chaos of the world. It's less than two square miles in size, so it's not hard to explore every corner of the island and get to know most of the locals (all 200 or so) in a few days.

Getting There

Needless to say, there's no airport on Mayreau — the nearest are on Union Island and Canouan. From Barbados, **Mustique Airways** and **TIA** fly to Union Island; from Grenada and Carriacou, **TIA** flies to Union. If you have prearranged a transfer with your Mayreau hotel, it is a short walk from the Union airport to the Anchorage Yacht Club dock, and a little farther to the Clifton docks. If your transfer is not prearranged, you'll need to walk into Clifton and hire a water taxi. The transfer should cost about $30 to $50, depending on your negotiating skills. **American Eagle** flies to Canouan from Barbados and San Juan. It's harder to hire a water taxi on the spot in Canouan, but there is the twice-weekly mail boat (see below).

Instead of hiring a water taxi, the other option is to use the MV Barracuda, the "mail boat" that makes the trip up and down the Grenadines twice a week. The ferry leaves St. Vincent on Monday, Thursday, and Saturday late morning and takes about four hours to reach Mayreau (stopping at Bequia and Canouan en route); the one-way fare is about $8. The Barracuda leaves Union (traveling north) on Tuesday and Friday mornings and Saturday afternoon, and the trip to Mayreau takes about 30 minutes (the ferry continues on to St. Vincent). Before traveling, be sure to confirm ferry times and days with the St. Vincent tourist office (784-457-1502).

Where to Stay

There are only two real choices on Mayreau, so the decision is not difficult. They are dramatically different from each other in both luxury and cost, but each will allow you to experience the best of what the island has to offer.

Saltwhistle Bay Club, Mayreau, St. Vincent and the Grenadines, W.I. ☎ 784-458-8444, ✆ 784-458-8944, ⌨ www.saltwhistle-bay.com, swbreserve@gmx.net

🛑 **Ridiculous** 🍽 **MAP** (closed September–October)

Located on what could be the most beautiful beach in the Grenadines, Saltwhistle Bay Club sits on 22 acres on the northern tip of the island. This is a private resort, enclosed by fences that help keep out the cows, donkeys, and other riffraff. There are 10 rooms in five double-unit cut stone cottages. Each room has either a king-size bed or twin beds. The decor is a bit on the dark side, with stone walls and dark mahogany closets and desks. This helps to keep the rooms cool even in the heat of the day and very pleasant at night. Each unit has a large airy bedroom with a sitting area, a circular stone shower, wooden shutters, and ceiling fans. The top of each unit is an open-air terrace the size of the whole building, great for relaxing and enjoying the sea breeze. There are hammocks that are strung between palm trees right outside your door. All you need is a rum punch and a good book.

Saltwhistle has its own restaurant, which serves breakfast, lunch, and dinner. The dining area is made up of individual circular stone tables and booths with thatched roofs that can fit six people comfortably. The chef of the restaurant is local and has created a balanced menu of international and regional cuisine.

Since the hotel is situated on the most amazing beach, known not only for 3,000 feet of the most incredible sand but also for the island's best anchorage, there are usually 10 to 20 yachts floating in the bay. Most of those folks stay on their boats, coming ashore only to enjoy the restaurant or the beach for a bit. Unfortunately, though, this is also a great spot for those annoying day-trippers. Undine Potter, the manager, does a great job of keeping them at bay (in the bay). They usually stay for only about an hour, and it's only a couple dozen people at the most. The swimming is amazing, as there is no coral reef inside the bay. If you get a chance, go for a skinny dip at night (better yet if it's a full moon). It's a little secret of Saltwhistle you won't ever forget!

For entertainment at the Saltwhistle, there is a steel drum band that plays on Thursdays. The band members come from another island in a boat on which most of us would never set foot. They pile in all their drums and five or six people and come over every week to entertain the "in town," but be prepared for a long walk up and down a hill. If you are going to go at night, ask Undine for a flashlight.

Saltwhistle offers snorkeling and fishing gear, windsurfing, and beach towels free to guests. There's good snorkeling at Saline Bay, around the wreck of the gunboat Piruna (kind of deep and a little rough). They can also arrange for other water sports, picnic trips to a small deserted islet, boat and yacht charters, and scuba diving.

Dennis' Hideaway, Mayreau, St. Vincent and the Grenadines, W.I. ⓒ 784-458-8594, ✆ same as phone, 🖳 www.dennis-hideaway.com, denhide@vincysurf.com

💲 Cheap ⑪ EP ⒸⒸ

Due to several rum punches offered at the bar by the ever-friendly and gregarious Dennis, our memory about his place is a tad blurry (and we can't even read our notes). However, we will try our best. Dennis' is located in the little village up the hill from Saline Bay. It's just off the road, tucked away in a pretty garden of local plants and flowers. There are five twin rooms, each with a private bathroom and a balcony. The rooms are clean, light, and airy, and all have a nice view of Saline Bay, but decor is minimal at best. There is a restaurant that serves breakfast, lunch, and dinner, with a Creole-style menu. Dennis's bar is frequented by locals as well as guests and visiting yachts.

Where to Eat

All the bars and restaurants are located in the village except for Salt-whistle Bay Club. With the exception of the latter, they are all within a few feet of each other. The night we were there, which was a Thursday, Dennis' Hideaway bar was busy and Island Paradise was packed. There was a Windjammer sailboat in the harbor, and most of the 60 to 70 passengers and crew were up in the village whooping it up.

$$ **Dennis' Hideaway**, 784-458-8594
       The Hideaway serves breakfast, lunch, and dinner. Great food and reasonably priced.

$$ **Island Paradise**, 784-458-8941
       This seems to be the hot spot on the island. We didn't get to eat here, but we hear that the food is very good. The place was

packed when we visited. There is a small dance floor with a jukebox playing a wide range of music, including reggae and island music. Everyone was dancing and drinking it up, including us! Note: The owner, James, has a cottage for rent. It is a self-contained two-bedroom unit, with running water, toilet, and kitchen. No electricity. **$ Dirt Cheap ⑪ EP**

$ **J & C Bar & Restaurant**, 784-458-8558
J & C serves a range of local and Creole foods along with cold drinks. The restaurant also has a small gift shop at Saltwhistle Bay, located right off the dock, where they sell cold drinks. This is great if you take the walk from the village over the hill to the beach at Saltwhistle. The hike can be very hot during the day (the path is not shaded), so you will welcome that cold drink when you get to the beach. It's also a great place to pick up a souvenir T-shirt.

$$ **Righteous**, 784-458-8071
This restaurant serves a variety of local foods. We love the name.

$$$$ **Saltwhistle Bay Club**, 784-458-8444
The restaurant serves international and Creole cuisine. Open for breakfast, lunch, and dinner (see Where to Stay review above).

Union Island

ONE OF THE SOUTHERNMOST OF ST. VINCENT'S GRENADINES, Union is perhaps the most topographically impressive island in the chain. Its profile of sheer peaks is unmistakable from a distance, rising dramatically to 999-foot Mt. Tobai. Coming in by plane is breathtaking as you swoop close to the mountains and then plunge to the short airstrip (sit on the left side for the best view). Alas, most of the island personality is owned by the Tahitian landscape. Otherwise, Union interacts with tourism primarily as a jumping-off point for Palm, Petit St. Vincent, and Mayreau. It also has a shady history as a transshipping axis for drugs, although we've never particularly observed this aspect. Note that our bags aroused more interest than usual when we arrived at the airport customs counter—we have no idea why.

Originally a cotton plantation, then used for subsistence farming, today Union Island thrives because of the yachting traffic. The Anchorage Yacht Club (see below) is the social hub of most visiting sailors. There are two villages: Ashton is primarily residential, whereas Clifton has most of the businesses. In Clifton you'll find a bank, several restaurants, a couple of hotels and Captain Yannis, who does day sails out of Union Island. Yannis does almost daily trips to the Tobago Cays, Mayreau, and Palm Island, and he is available for charters. Call for reservations, 784-458-8513, or check the Web site, www.captainyannis.com.

It's a 20-minute walk from Ashton to Clifton. In fact, walking is a great way to explore the island—there are unpaved tracks on the west coast of the island that offer wonderful views, and Chatham Bay is beautiful and undeveloped. There are usually a few yachts anchored in crescent-shaped Chatham, but the swimming is better at Big Sand (aka Belmont Bay), which has just a few buildings nearby.

There is also a trail up to the striking Pinnacles, which offers the island's best view.

If you choose to stay a night or two, there's a tourist office in Clifton, but they have little to offer beyond a few brochures. When we asked what activities there were to do on Union, the young woman behind the counter said: "Well, you can take a day sail to the Tobago Cays." When we explained that we had just come from there, she seemed stumped to offer something of interest on Union. Granted, the scene in Clifton is nothing terribly appealing, so don't plan on staying too long. However, if you are on a modest budget and want to sample several of the remote Grenadines, then Union is a good base for your explorations.

Getting There

The gateway to Union is Barbados, and **Mustique Airways** and **TIA** have daily flights. **Mustique Airways** and **SVG Air** also have flights from the northern Grenadines and St. Vincent, while **TIA** connects Grenada and Carriacou to Union, and **Air Caraibes** flies in from Martinique. You can also take the "mail boat" from St. Vincent, the MV Barracuda. The ferry leaves St. Vincent on Monday, Thursday, and Saturday, late morning, and takes about five hours to reach Union (stopping at Bequia, Canouan, and Mayreau en route); the one-way fare is $15. The Barracuda leaves Union (traveling north) on Tuesday and Friday mornings and Saturday afternoon. Before traveling, be sure to confirm ferry times and days with the St. Vincent tourist office (784-457-1502). There is also limited boat service between Carriacou and Union on Monday and Thursday—confirm with the tourist office.

Where to Stay

Anchorage Yacht Club Hotel & Marina, Union Island, St. Vincent and the Grenadines, W.I. ℂ 784-458-8221, ✆ 784-458-8365, 🖳 ww.ayc-hotel-grenadines.com, ofc@ayc-hotel-grenadines.com

- 💼 **Cheap** for the standard rooms and **Not So Cheap** for the others ⑪ **EP** (closed September through mid-October)

This outfit has a very "Don't Stop the Carnival" ambiance, with questionable service and 15 less-than-primped rooms. Nonetheless, longtime manager Charlotte Honnart does her best to make your stay on Union memorable. There are three types of units, all of which boast sea views. Four cabanas in a low-slung block have a good amount of space and are air-conditioned; each has a semiprivate outdoor shower (more functional than exotic). There are six standard rooms in the main building above the restaurant; upkeep is shoddy. There are five bungalows that are a short walk away from the main complex — these have air conditioning and a modicum of Robinson Crusoe escapist air, but little in the way of traditional polish (they feel a little forgotten). Along the waterfront is the restaurant, which is fronted by a pen containing nurse sharks. The dining is popular with visiting yachties, but we found breakfast to be overpriced and underwhelming — we threw our toast to the sharks.

Clifton Beach Hotel, Union Island, St. Vincent and the Grenadines, W.I. ℭ 784-458-8235, ✎ 784-458-8313, 🖳 www.cliftonbeach-hotel.com, clifbeachhotel@caribsurf.com

🔹 **Cheap ⑪ EP ⒸⒸ**

Anchorage may be the better known, slightly more polished operation, but this spot has one of our favorite rooms in the Grenadines: room 26, on the third floor. It is open to the breeze on three sides and looks directly out to the water and a scene of bobbing masts. It's really sweet. Other rooms are nowhere near as nice, but they're adequate if you're just passing through for the night. Expect little in the way of traditional hotel services.

Where to Eat

$$$ **Anchorage Yacht Club,** Clifton, 784-458-8221
Pretty standard island fare, but pricey for what you get. There's a "jump-up" with a live steel band on Mondays and Fridays.

$$ **Captain Gourmet,** Clifton, 784-458-8918
A French-owned deli with fresh baked breads, sandwiches, decent wine, and imported canned goods. No seating, but it is a little dollop of take-away refinement for the visiting boat crews.

$$ **Lambi's,** Clifton, 784-458-8549
This is a good spot to take in the local cuisine, particularly the titular item (aka conch), and other fresh seafood, all prepared Caribbean style.

Petite Martinique

TOURISTO SCALE

THIS ODD LITTLE OUTPOST IS PART OF GRENADA'S GRE-
nadines, although its residents hardly think so. While we didn't exactly spot an independence movement during our visit to the island,
there's definitely an autonomous streak running under the surface.
Located three miles northeast of Carriacou, this 486-acre blip on the
radar screen is inhabited by about 900 or so residents of predomi-
nantly French descent. They live at the base of a 738-foot extinct volcanic cone, and there are about two dozen cars on the island to tool
about the half-mile or so of road. There are some odd looking trac-
tors or dumpsters that ferry goods from the dock up to homes, and
many people own a speedboat. It's safe to say they don't use them
just for pleasure cruises.

Petite Martinique—also known as PM—has a much higher
standard of living than its neighbors. This is largely due to its
proudly held position as the smuggling capital of the West Indies, a
decades-old tradition that was probably born from the lack of a customs official. Today it is common to see Carriacou-built trading boats
laden with Sony Wega TVs, refrigerators, and Bordeaux wine coming
from *gros* Martinique, St. Martin, and Guadeloupe. Need an outboard
motor for your boat? One Grenadian priest told us how he saved
hundreds of dollars by purchasing his on PM. Although the admin-
istration in Grenada cracks down on the contraband from time to
time, they probably realize that if they were ever to really snuff out
the trafficking, they'd have a bigger headache dealing with the hundreds of unemployed islanders.

There's a bank that's open for a few hours three days a week, a
scruffy shell-laden beach that curls around the town (fair for swimming, but not for sunning), and you can hike to the summit of the
island in about 30 minutes—the view is great. There's a disco at

Melodies on weekends. Otherwise, that's about it. In short, we wouldn't spend the night here, but it's fine as a diversion for a few hours from PSV or Carriacou.

Getting There

There's no airport—the nearest is on Carriacou, which is served from Grenada and Barbados (see the Carriacou chapter for details). The Osprey ferry travels to PM on Monday through Friday via Carriacou, leaving Grenada at 9 a.m. and 5:30 p.m., stopping at Carriacou at 10:30 a.m. and 7 p.m., arriving on PM at 11 a.m. and 7:30 p.m., respectively. The return trip leaves PM at 5:30 a.m. and 3 p.m., arriving on Grenada two hours later. The Saturday and Sunday schedule is slightly reduced. The fare from Grenada is $16 each way, or $4 from Carriacou. It's also possible to hire a water taxi in Windwardside on Carriacou.

Where to Stay

Melodies Guest House, Petite Martinique, Grenada, W.I.
     © 473-443-9052, ✆ 473-443-9093, 🖥 www.spiceisle.com/melodies, melodies@caribsurf.com
  💰 **Dirt Cheap** 🍴 **EP** ㏄

     Although there are a couple of places to stay overnight, this is probably the best. The 10 rooms are found on the second floor of a beachfront building. All are basic but clean and decent for the price. There's a restaurant and a dance hall downstairs.

Where to Eat

$$ **Palm Beach,** 473-443-9103
     Located almost next to the boat dock, this serves an inviting menu of grilled fish, jerk chicken, rôti, and a variety of shrimp dishes.

Palm Island

TOURISTO SCALE

BAREFOOT VACATION FANTASIES MAY COME TO LIFE ON this rather quirky outpost located just east of Union Island. The drawing card is gently rustling palms and powdery white sand beach, and a single, recently revamped resort that gives the all-inclusive experience a fresh spin.

Getting There

From Barbados, **Mustique Airways** and **TIA** fly to Union Island; from Grenada, **TIA** flies to Union. **Mustique Airways** and **SVG Air** also have flights from the northern Grenadines and St. Vincent. Once on Union, a Palm Island representative will escort you from the airport to a nearby dock at the Anchorage Hotel and then on to the island via private launch. The boat ride takes about 10 minutes.

Where to Stay and Eat

Palm Island, Palm Island, St. Vincent and the Grenadines, W.I.
ⓒ Stateside: 800-345-0356, Local: 784-458-8824, 📠 784-458-8804, 🖥 www.palmislandresorts.com, res@palmislandresorts.com

💲 **Stratospheric** 🍽 **All-inclusive** (does not include any off-island activities) Ⓒ

Originally the unappealingly-named Prune Island, entrepreneur John Caldwell purchased a 198-year lease to this 130-acre spot back in the 1960s and renamed it Palm Island, planted a few thousand palms trees and eventually built a beachfront resort by hand. Over the years, Caldwell began to lease plots to individuals to build private homes on the island, but eventually the hotel became run-down. In 1999 the hotel was sold to Elite Island Resorts, a Florida-based operator of all-inclusive hotels, most of them on the island of Antigua. After $4 million in renovations, Palm Island was refashioned into a high-end, all-inclusive luxury operation. A key difference between Palm and Petit St. Vincent (which follows — the two are just a couple of miles from each other) is that two dozen homeowners have villas on the island. Palm's pretty beaches are also visited by yachts and smaller cruise ships, whereas PSV manages to keep most of these offshore. But the villas are rarely occupied, so mostly you'll be sharing Palm with the guests of the 37-room resort. Fortunately, there are no cars, just a few golf carts, not that you'll need any wheels to get across the island — nothing is farther than a 15-minute walk.

Overall, the renovations have done much to improve the experience. Four types of accommodations are available: Palm View rooms are the least expensive, and have louvered windows, en suite bathrooms, walls of bluebitch stone, and ceilings made of attractive woven thatch. They may be the bottom of the rate card, but these are perfectly fine. Beachfront rooms are similar, if a tad smaller, but with a beach view. Plantation Suites are in a two-story block of four, set back slightly from the beach, but with a huge lanai (second-floor units have views and slightly more privacy). Last, there are Island Lofts, which are perched on stilts about five feet off the ground and have huge bathrooms and cathedral ceilings. One kink that is still being worked out is air conditioning — Palm has stand-alone units that sit on the floor. These have the advantage of keeping machine noise down *outside* the room (a big plus), but they don't do a great job of cooling down the room, and they aren't exactly quiet next to your bed. We turned ours off and opened the screened windows to let the island breezes do their trick, which worked just fine. Several guests during our visit made the AC units their one and only complaint.

All rooms have ceiling fans, rattan and bamboo furniture, Egyptian cotton bed linens, room safes, bathrobes, and attractive original sea-themed artwork by Palm's resident artist, Patrick Chevailler, a French doctor who lives for much of the year on the island. Amenities include room service, tea and coffee maker, a stocked fridge (water, soft drinks, and beer only). There are no phones or TVs in the rooms. The island is wrapped by white-sand beaches, and there is excellent snorkeling available. Tennis and croquet are available, and there's a tour desk to set up day trips (at an additional cost). There are two restaurants, and meals are better than we've experienced at most all-inclusive operations—this is probably in part due to the attentive oversight of general manager Julian G. Waterer, formerly the chef and owner of Julian's restaurant in Antigua. The generous swimming pool looks a little awkward, what with its waterfall plunging from a faux summit, but it's also a good place to hang out if the beach gets busy (not that it happens often).

We think that Palm makes a good vacation for those who really want to get away from it all: TV, phones, traffic, noise. You'll find none of it here. You'll want to bring some reading material, and also don't forget to budget in some time for an excursion to the splendid Tobago Cays.

Petit St. Vincent

LOOKING FOR THE "PRIVATE ISLAND" EXPERIENCE, WHERE every square inch of terra firma beneath your feet is "yours"—at least until check-out comes? Then check out Petit St. Vincent, perhaps the Caribbean's original private island resort, located just a stone's throw from the Grenada/St. Vincent border (St. Vincent side), but where border ministrations are a non-issue and a barefoot informality is the rule.

Getting There

From Barbados, **Mustique Airways** and **TIA** fly to Union Island; from Grenada, **TIA** flies to Union. **Mustique Airways** and **SVG Air** also have flights from the northern Grenadines and St. Vincent. Once on Union, a Petit St. Vincent representative will escort you from the airport to a nearby dock at the Anchorage Hotel, and then on to the island via private launch. The boat ride takes about 30 minutes.

Where to Stay and Eat

⊛ **Petit St. Vincent Resort (PSV)**, Petit St. Vincent, St. Vincent and the Grenadines, W.I. ℂ Stateside: 800-654-9326 or 954-963-7401, ✆ 954-963-7402, Local: 784-458-8801, ✆ 784-458-8428, 🖥 www.psvresort.com, info@psvresort.com

   💲 **Stratospheric** ⑪ **FAP** ⒸⒸ (closed every September–October)

   When the boat launch for PSV (as Petit St. Vincent is affectionately called) picked us up, we knew we were headed someplace special. Piloted by Maurice, a very friendly man dressed in a white uniform (which looked like formal military dress to us), the boat whisked us away to our very own private island. That is exactly what it is: a very secluded resort nestled on a privately owned 113-acre island. It has just 22 cottages (three double units) sparsely dispersed about the island, each with its own discreet view of the ocean. Some of the cottages are right on the beach, some are tucked away on the hillside, and a couple are located on the far side of the island. All are extremely private. Each cut-stone and dark-wood cottage has a living room with two sofas (they can be turned into daybeds), a bedroom (with two queen-size beds), dressing room, bathroom with shower, and private patio with a hammock. All have ceiling fans, louvered windows, and terra-cotta-tiled floors. The stone walls (including the floor and walls of the shower) help to keep the rooms cool, even in the heat of the day. The fabrics are tropical pink-and-green (à la Gloria Upson and Bunny Bixley), exuding a faded elegance. We found the beds and pillows comfortable. There were soft cotton towels, plush robes, and Crabtree & Evelyn toiletries, too. Conspicuously absent are TVs, air conditioning, and phones.

So how do you communicate with the resort? PSV has devised an ingenious system. Outside the cottage is a flagpole with two colored flags, red and yellow. If room service is desired, a written note is placed in the bamboo tube at the base of the pole and the yellow flag is raised. A member of the staff should be by within 20 minutes (they are constantly circling the island in minimokes). If you do not want to be disturbed, raise the red flag. Trust us—and we tested this—if you raise the red one, you will not be disturbed for any reason. Privacy is valued on PSV (trysters take note)!

The service is excellent. With more than 75 staff members to accommodate the needs of 44 guests, your needs will be met. The dining pavilion (if you don't opt for room service) is located in the main complex. We loved the open-air dining experience for all meals. Breakfast is standard fare, with nice touches of local fruits, vegetables, home-baked breads, and pastries. Lunch is served buffet style with both hot and cold dishes such as seafood, pasta, sandwiches, fruit, and desserts. Dinner is informal, but men tend to wear trousers (not shorts) and the women dresses (we sometimes get into dressing up a little, even on vacation). The dinner menu was a good fusion of international and Caribbean cuisine, using local seafood, fruits, and vegetables from St. Vincent; and other fine foods from the U.S. (like real Vermont maple syrup). PSV boasts its own bakery and pastry chef, and, we have to admit, the homemade stuff was great.

If swimming and sunbathing are the only things on your agenda, PSV will oblige, with two miles of white-sand beaches, all within a short walk or ride in a minimoke. The windward beaches have great snorkeling and stay relatively cool, thanks to the trade winds. The beach on the west side of the island has palapas (thatched-roof mini-pavilions), and the kitchen will pack a picnic lunch and arrange for a minimoke to give you a ride. There is now a yellow flagpole service on the west side beach. They have also added toilets and a shower—more time to spend lazing around, reading, snorkeling, or just sleeping. Chances are you won't find another soul within eyesight. The staff will check on you periodically for supplies (i.e. water, suntan lotion, food, or a ride back).

PSV also offers water sports, including Hobie Cats, Sunfish, windsurfers, and snorkeling equipment, and there is a 20-station fitness trail for those seeking some exercise. Just walking around the island is fun, too (the trip is about two miles and will take you about an hour). We started our walk late in the day, and as we came around the northern tip of the island into Conch Bay, we witnessed the most amazing sunset. There is a lighted tennis court (complete with racquets and balls at no charge), and we actually saw people using it. Scuba-diving excursions to nearby islands can also be arranged.

Two things we will always remember about PSV are the sky at night—with its millions of stars shining brighter than anything we've seen up north—and the sound of the waves as they gently lulled us to sleep.

St. Vincent

MILES

FANCY

FALLS OF
BALEINE

CARIBBEAN SEA

SANDY BAY

LA SOUFRIÉRE
▲(3,864 FT.)

TRINITY
FALLS

RICHMOND
BEACH

CHATEAUBELAIR

GEORGETOWN

SPRING
VILLAGE

WALLILABOU BAY

BARROUALLIE

GRAND
BONBOMME
▲

NORTH
UNION

ATLANTIC
OCEAN

PARROT
RESERVE

LAYOU

VERMONT

BIABOU

PETIT
BYAHAUT

MESOPOTAMIA

BOTANICAL
GARDEN

KINGSTOWN

HERON

VILLA

AIRPORT

KINGSTOWN PARK INN

GRAND VIEW BEACH HOTEL

YOUNG
ISLAND

MARINERS

UMBRELLA BEACH APTS.

FERRY TO BEQUIA

BEQUIA

St. Vincent

OTHER ISLANDS CLAIM TO PRESERVE THE CARIBBEAN THE way it used to be; St. Vincent actually lives it. The somewhat ramshackle capital, Kingstown, has weathered wooden guest houses and a colorful marketplace with gaping fish and colorful fruit for sale; cruise ships and their passengers are not part of the scene. An agricultural economy predominates, large portions of St. Vincent remain undeveloped, and there are no real white-sand beaches, so the island has minimal tourism infrastructure. Most visitors are steered to the nearby Grenadines, to which St. Vincent is linked politically. They have more conventional tourist appeal, the government reasons, so the main island is left relatively untouched. When producers of the movie White Squall were looking for a spot that could represent the West Indies of the 1960s, they chose St. Vincent for much of their location shooting.

The flip side of this seeming bucolia is that the island is struggling under the weight of its banana-based economy. The World Trade Organization has taken the side of the United States (and American banana-exporting companies) in its "banana war" with the European Union (which has been trying to protect the banana exports of their former colonies). Further, the U.S. has devoted plenty of manpower toward eradicating a certain leafy herb (canonized by Cheech & Chong and a popular export to the U.S.) from Vincentian soil. Considering that these two items are the number one and (probably) number two cash crops on the island, this double whammy has not endeared Americans to locals, and it can be felt in the somewhat brusque interactions that have become commonplace.

That said, adventurous travelers who head off the beaten path will find dramatic scenery, great hiking, a good array of less expensive

St. Vincent: Key Facts

Location	13°N by 60°W
	2,040 miles (3,283 km) southeast of New York
	100 miles (161 km) west of Barbados
	75 miles (121 km) north of Grenada
Size	133 square miles (344 square km)
Highest point	La Soufrière, 4,048 feet (1234 m)
Population	100,000
Language	English
Time	Atlantic Standard Time (1 hour ahead of EST, same as EDT)
Area code	784
Electricity	220 volts AC, 50 cycles, so you'll need to bring an adapter and transformer for laptops and electric shavers
Currency	The Eastern Caribbean dollar, EC$ (EC$2.68 = US$1)
Driving	On the LEFT; you'll need a temporary permit. Just present your valid U.S. or Canadian driver's license and pay the $28 fee (!) for a local license.
Departure tax	$13
Documents	U.S. and Canadian citizens must have a passport; all visitors must hold a return or ongoing ticket.
Beer to drink	Hairoun
Rum to drink	Any Vincentian brand
Music to hear	Dancehall
Tourism info	800-729-1726
	www.svgtourism.com

hotels, and real West Indian charm. All of this adds up to a pretty special package: an island that shows few of the scars from modern tourism that some of its neighbors wear. It may be one of the last West Indian islands to be stepping into the 21st century, but St. Vincent has an irresistible backwater appeal that is getting hard to find in the increasingly packaged-for-the-masses Caribbean.

The Briefest History

St. Vincent's first residents were the Ciboney Indians, who arrived by canoe from South America and were followed by the Arawaks and then the Caribs. The latter were a tenacious bunch and overwhelmed their predecessors. Columbus cruised by St. Vincent in 1498, although historians are unsure as to whether he actually saw the island, let alone came ashore. Legend has it that the Caribs were ferocious enough to keep subsequent explorers away for almost two centuries (those who visited the island did not find a red carpet rolled out). In the late 1700s, the Caribs, British, and French battled for control of St. Vincent; in fact, as the Caribs were defeated on neighboring islands, survivors made their way to St. Vincent, swelling the Indian ranks. Then escaped slaves from Barbados sailed to St. Vincent and mixed with the Indians to form a fierce tribe known as the Black Caribs. The Europeans and Indians fought for control of the island for decades, until 1797, when the British successfully dominated the Black Caribs and deported 5,000 of their ranks to the island of Roatan (near Honduras) — not a very PC maneuver. The remaining Caribs retreated to the northeast shore of the island (a few descendants of the Caribs still live there, and the Caribbean Organization of Indigenous People is based on St. Vincent). Britain granted St. Vincent statehood in 1979; today it is an independent state within the British Commonwealth.

Getting There

St. Vincent's small E.T. Joshua Airport can be reached only from nearby islands. **LIAT** and **Caribbean Star** fly to St. Vincent from neighboring islands including Antigua, Barbados, Grenada, St. Lucia, and Trinidad. **TIA, SVG Air** and **Mustique Airways** fly in from the Grenadines and Barbados. St. Vincent's airport is conveniently located between Kingstown, the capital, and Villa, the primary hotel area — within a ten-minute drive of each.

Getting Around

The good news is that almost all of St. Vincent's hotels and restaurants are concentrated around the island's southern tip. The bad news is that the roads are rough and driving is on the left. However, there are a few small car-rental firms on the island; try **David's Auto Clinic** in Kingstown (784-456-4026), **Ben's Auto Rental** near the airport (784-456-2907), or **Unico Auto Rentals** at the airport (784-456-5744), and **Avis Rent-a-Car** at the airport and in Kingstown (800-331-1212 or 784-456-2929). Prices are high, starting at about $45 per day. A taxi ride from the airport to any of the hotels in Kingstown or Villa is $7.50.

If you just want to spend a day sightseeing, it may be easier to hire a taxi. We've had good luck with **Sam's Taxi Tours**: 784-456-4338. Alternatively, you can use the local minibus service, particularly for trips between the Villa area and Kingstown. Fares are rarely higher than $2. For travel into the Grenadines via speedboat, contact **Fantasea Tours**, located in Villa opposite Young Island: 784-457-4477.

Focus on St. Vincent:
The Hike to La Soufrière ⊛

This is a day trip that will both please and exhaust the most energetic — a hike up the Soufrière volcano on the northern end of the island. Other than Montserrat's English Crater, in recent years St. Vincent's Soufrière has been the region's most actively monitored volcano; an eruption in 1902 caused 2,000 deaths, and in 1979, 20,000 were evacuated when the crater rumbled to life and deposited a layer of ash across the northern half of the island (everyone returned home safe and sound that time). The flip side of this is that La Soufrière keeps St. Vincent lush, green, and fertile (the ash makes for great soil). The volcano has been relatively quiet for the last couple of decades, so pack up your good walking shoes, water, energy snack, and a windbreaker or sweatshirt. It's cool and windy at the top, and after the sweaty hike it will make your teeth chatter.

The traditional route to the summit climbs the eastern slope above Georgetown, about an hour's drive from Kingstown (another trail ascends the slopes from Richmond on the west side, but it is more arduous). From the Rabacca Dry River just beyond George-town, watch for the road that leads up through banana and coconut plantations. After about two miles on this rutted road, you'll reach the trailhead. From here it is a three-hour, fairly strenuous hike through bamboo forests and along misty ridges to the crater rim and summit. And rim is no exaggeration. You actually crawl up to the edge of the crater and peer over a sheer lip that drops hundreds of feet to the floor of the volcano. There used to be a rather large lake in the crater, but it is now only a semblance of its former self. If you walk carefully along the rim to the right from the top of the path, you will find a rope pegged into the ground. It was put here by scientists who go down to take measurements on the activity deep inside the mountain. You can climb down via the rope (with some sort of pro-tection for your hands) to roam around the crater floor. Before doing this, tug on it a few times to make sure it's in good shape, and avoid putting your full weight on the rope (otherwise you might end up as a postscript on the hometown 11 o'clock news). Obviously, the climb back up to the crater rim is very tiring — before heading down, think whether you have the energy for the return trip. After you've taken your pictures and refueled, the trip back down the main trail will be easier, and if you've been lucky enough to tackle the summit on a clear day, you'll come home with great pictures, too.

It is possible to hike La Soufrière on your own (the trail is rela-tively easy to follow), but a well-versed guide will provide valuable in-sight into the lush flora and fauna on the way up. Clint and Mildred Hazell at **Hazeco Tours** (784-457-8634) are your best bet, and they also offer birdwatching trips, excursions to the waterfalls, and more (see below).

What Else to See

Less strenuous hiking trips visit other interesting sights on St. Vin-cent. The Vermont Forest Nature Trail climbs through the Buccament Valley, home to the endangered and beautiful St. Vincent parrot, a dazzling brown-and-gold bird with a white head and tail feathers sporting a rainbow of colors. There are only about 500 in the wild, but conservation efforts are beginning to pay off. The trailhead is just above the town of Vermont and leads to a 1.5-mile loop that traverses the serene tropical rain forest on the slopes of 3,000-foot Grand Bonhomme. There's a viewing area halfway around the loop, and at dawn or just before sunset you have a good chance of spotting the parrots winging through.

Another worthwhile hike visits ⊛**Trinity Falls,** set deep in a lush canyon below La Soufrière's western flank. The trailhead is found by driving the leeward coast road through Chateaubelair to the Richmond Vale Academy, where a side road leads about a mile farther, eventually to become a four-wheel-drive track. Follow this path into the valley to the falls, about a 45-minute trek. A hot spring, which emerged after the 1979 eruption of La Soufrière, is a recent addition to the remote canyon. Another waterfall that's even more isolated is the Falls of Baleine, located on the north coast of the island and reachable only by boat. The 60-foot falls aren't as impressive as Trinity, but on a clear day the boat trip along these undeveloped shores can be quite invigorating.

Kingstown is worth at least a half-day of exploration. Of particular note is the Botanical Gardens, which are located on a hillside just north of town. This 20-acre garden is the oldest in the Western Hemisphere, dating back to 1765. You'll find teak, mahogany, and cannonball trees, as well as breadfruit trees descended from the seedlings brought over by Captain Bligh. About three dozen St. Vincent parrots are found here in an aviary toward the back of the garden; the up-close scrutiny of these stunning birds is a rare privilege. Also check out St. Mary's Catholic Cathedral, an unexpected blend of Romanesque, Moorish, and Georgian architecture that was built in 1823. Market Square, right next to the harbor, bustles with activity on Fridays and Saturdays—quite photogenic, but remember to ask before snapping photos.

St. Vincent isn't known for its beaches, and the best ones are those of black sand. There are a number along the west coast, and the one at Wallilabou is particularly attractive; also try Cumberland Bay and remote Richmond Beach. Around Villa there are slivers of gray-brown beaches. Although these are sufficient for swimming, they aren't much to get excited about. If white-sand beaches are a prerequisite, head to Bequia or the other Grenadines.

Where to Stay

Accommodations on St. Vincent are concentrated between Kingstown and Villa, the mostly residential area facing Young Island.

Young Island, P.O. Box 211, Young Island, St. Vincent, W.I.
  ℂ Stateside: 800-223-1108, Local: 784-458-4826, ✆ 784-457-4567, 🖳 www.youngisland.com, reservations@youngisland.com
  💰 **Ridiculous** ⓘ **MAP** ⒸⒸ

If it's luxury you want, there's Young Island, the closest thing to a real resort "on" St. Vincent. Calling it a private island resort is a bit of an exaggeration: a Chappaquiddick-size swim, and you're practically in downtown Kingstown. Nevertheless, it is one of those service-and-sunshine places that are à la mode for some. In fact, Young's prices are a fair notch below those of other private island resorts in the Caribbean, so it does represent good value.

The hotel sits on a 35-acre rock located about 200 yards off St. Vincent's Villa area. There's a trifling, some would say charming, boat that chugs back and forth across the channel all day. The 30 rooms are in rock-walled cottages cooled by trade winds and ceiling fans; the decor has been spruced up, and the rooms are spacious and fairly private, with outdoor showers wrapped in volcanic stone and vines. Some are just above the water, others clamber over the rock, and three have private plunge pools. Diversions include tennis, a tropical pool, hammocks, a smallish white-sand beach with a swim-up bar floating just offshore, and nonmotorized water sports. There is also a pair of 44-foot yachts available for overnight trips in the Grenadines—a good way to combine a resort and sailing vacation. Food is reliably good, if unspectacular, and service is attentive.

Grand View Beach Hotel, P.O. Box 173, Villa Point, St. Vincent, W.I. ℂ Stateside: 800-223-6510, Local: 784-458-4811, ℘ 784-457-4174, ▭ www.grandviewhotel.com, granview@caribsurf.com

🛅 Pricey ⑪ EP ⒸⒸ

This former cotton plantation house sits on a dramatic lava bluff overlooking Young Island and the beach at Villa—the setting lives up to the hotel's name, although the beach is pretty marginal. The 19 rooms are not dressy but are decent, and some have nice views from their balconies. There's a very good restaurant serving island fare, tennis and squash courts, a well-appointed fitness center, and a small pool, and we love the contemporary art collection that has started to materialize on the walls. Open since 1964, the Grand View is well connected to the local political scene and is mainland St. Vincent's best-run property. Rates are a little high for what you get in terms of lodging, but we've always found the welcome of owner Tony Sardine and his staff to be most hospitable.

Mariner's, Villa Beach, St. Vincent, W.I. ℂ Stateside: 800-223-1108, Local: 784-457-7000, ℘ 784-457-4333, ▭ www.marinershotel.com, marinershotel@caribsurf.com

🛅 Not So Cheap ⑪ EP ⒸⒸ

Also facing Young Island, this 20-room inn was smartly refurbished in 1997 and packs quite a lot of style into its small property and reasonable rates. All rooms are bright and spacious, with air conditioning, cable TV, and a balcony. Watersports and excursions are nearby. There is no beach, but the small shoreside swimming pool offers nice views.

Umbrella Beach Apartments, Villa Beach, St. Vincent, W.I. ℂ 784-458-4651, ℘ 784-457-4930

🛅 Cheap ⑪ EP ⒸⒸ

These are charming but rundown accommodations. A favorite of those on the guest-house circuit, the nine rooms at this establishment have private baths and kitchenettes. It's a good location on the water, and water sports are available. Several restaurants are a short walk away.

Kingstown Park Inn, P.O. Box 1594, Kingstown, St. Vincent, W.I. ✆ 784-457-2964, ✉ 784-457-2505

📠 **Dirt Cheap** 🍴 **EP** cc

Located on a hill overlooking Kingstown and Bequia beyond, this converted old plantation house gets raves from guests. The seven quarters are clean and cheap, and good West Indian cuisine is served. It's only about a ten-minute walk into town and is less than three miles from the airport.

The Heron, P.O. Box 430, Kingstown, St. Vincent, W.I. ✆ 784-457-1631, ✉ 784-457-1189

📠 **Cheap** 🍴 **CP** cc

An easy walk from the ferry dock, this is a great spot to stay if you want to catch the early boat to Bequia. The comfortable rooms — in paler tones with uneven wood floors surrounding a courtyard — provide refuge from the not-very-scenic neighborhood. A classic West Indian guest house, with a decent restaurant downstairs (you'll smell the curry in your room at lunch).

Petit Byahaut, Petit Byahaut, St. Vincent, W.I. ✆ 784-457-7008, ✉ same as phone, 🖥 outahere.com/petitbyahaut, petitbyahaut@caribsurf.com

📠 **Ridiculous** (includes water sports, guided hikes, airport transfer — three-night minimum required) 🍴 **FAP** cc

If you want to stay in a pristine 50-acre valley that is accessible only by boat, try this crunchy establishment, where your room is a 10-by-13-foot floored tent with screened windows, queen-size bed, solar-heated outdoor shower, and hammock. Rates include all meals and activities (including snorkeling, kayaking, and Sunfish sailboats). There's a safari-style atmosphere (minus the big game), but this is a love-it-or-hate-it spot that seems way overpriced to us.

Where to Eat

Despite the setting, St. Vincent is not a culinary paradise, although things are improving. Here's the best of a mediocre bunch.

$ **Aggie's**, Kingstown, 784-456-2110
An informal lunch spot with a good West Indian selection, including rôti, conch souse, curried beef or mutton, and pumpkin or callaloo soup.

$$$ **Basil's Bar and Restaurant**, Kingstown, 784-457-2597
The name of Mustique fame, this is a colorful island hangout with an all-you-can-eat buffet at lunch, and lobster, filet mignon, and grilled red snapper at dinner.

$$$$ ⊛ **Lime Restaurant**, Villa, 784-458-4227
Probably the island's most popular hangout, though a bit overpriced. Dinner menu includes grilled steaks, fish, and lobster (live in season, September-April). The local yachties tell us to try the African black pepper steak. There's also a cheaper pub menu available for lunch and dinner.

$ **Nice Food**, Kingstown, 784-456-1391
Situated beneath the Heron, a classic guest house near the ferry dock, this spot serves a full English breakfast or buffet Creole lunches.

$$$ **Pebbles**, Ra-wa-cou, 784-458-0190
Noel Frasier runs this unexpected find on the east coast of the island, above a small beach at Mount Pleasant. Frasier used to cook at American resorts and maintains an organic veggie garden for much of his produce. You'll find international dishes. Reservations required.

$ **Vee Jay's**, Kingstown, 784-457-2845
This is a good place for a West Indian lunch while you're touring the capital. It's located on Upper Bay Street.

$$$$ **Young Island**, Villa, 784-458-4826
The food is not stellar, but this is the place for a special meal

(assuming you're not ensconced at Young Island already). The West Indian buffet on Wednesday and barbecue on Saturday are popular ($45 per person). Other nights, look for a limited entrée selection, served in a pretty open-air setting just off the beach.

Don't Miss

✪ La Soufrière

The trek to the summit is one of the Caribbean's top hikes. The volcano has a major blow about once a century, so catch it while it's still sleeping.

Vermont Nature Trails

A beautiful valley that is the most likely place to see the St. Vincent parrot in the wild, as well as iguana and armadillo.

The Botanical Gardens

The gardens are fair, but this is your best bet to see the St. Vincent parrot up close.

Bequia

Even if you're only on a day trip, this is one of the region's most appealing hangouts, and it's easy to reach on the regular ferry from Kingstown. Be sure to bring along your bathing suit.

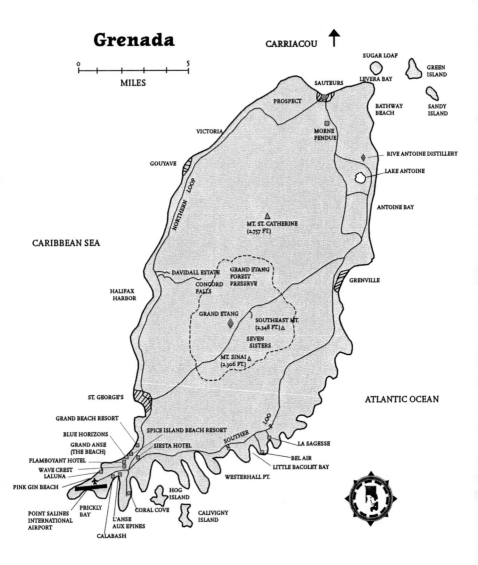

Grenada

CARRIACOU

MILES
0 5

SUGAR LOAF
LEVERA BAY
GREEN ISLAND
SANDY ISLAND

SAUTEURS

BATHWAY BEACH

PROSPECT

VICTORIA

MORNE FENDUE

RIVE ANTOINE DISTILLERY

GOUYAVE

LAKE ANTOINE

NORTHERN LOOP

ANTOINE BAY

MT. ST. CATHERINE
(2,757 FT.)

CARIBBEAN SEA

DAVIDALL ESTATE

GRAND ETANG FOREST PRESERVE

CONCORD FALLS

GRENVILLE

HALIFAX HARBOR

GRAND ETANG

SOUTHEAST MT.
(2,348 FT.)

SEVEN SISTERS

MT. SINAI
(2,306 FT.)

ST. GEORGE'S

ATLANTIC OCEAN

GRAND BEACH RESORT

LOOP

BLUE HORIZONS

SPICE ISLAND BEACH RESORT

GRAND ANSE (THE BEACH)

SIESTA HOTEL

SOUTHER

LA SAGESSE

FLAMBOYANT HOTEL

BEL AIR

WAVE CREST
LALUNA

LITTLE BACOLET BAY

PINK GIN BEACH

WESTERHALL PT.

HOG ISLAND

POINT SALINES INTERNATIONAL AIRPORT

PRICKLY BAY

CORAL COVE

CALIVIGNY ISLAND

L'ANSE AUX EPINES

CALABASH

Grenada

GRENADA IS WONDERFULLY EVOCATIVE. NICKNAMED THE "Isle of Spice," the land is redolent with the cloves, allspice, cinnamon, and, especially, nutmeg that grow throughout its hillsides. The island's tranquil natural assets of lush tropical vegetation, gushing rivers, scenic mountains, and coastline are powerful and do much to overcome the memory of political turmoil and a brash American invasion in 1983.

Grenada is a great place to visit if you want to hike and immerse yourself in its people and past. The country still has a bantam, out-of-the-way disposition, which makes the island a good choice for vacationers who don't care to follow in the footsteps of a million cruise-ship passengers. There is one excellent beach (Grand Anse) and a trove of smaller coves, and the island's rugged interior beckons with hiking opportunities. Outside the primary tourist areas of Grand Anse, L'Anse aux Epines, and St. George's (the capital), you begin to experience the real Grenada. Vivid images come to mind of women washing clothes in a river, potholed roads, spice stations, rich hues of green, and the ever watchful eyes of the people, who are among the region's friendliest hosts.

The country (which includes the neighboring islands of Carriacou and Petit Martinique to the north) is a popular destination for Europeans, particularly Germans, Brits, and Italians, but Americans are increasingly discovering this special island. Most who visit here rarely venture into the interior of the island, which is a shame for them. Grenada appeals to the adventurous traveler (our readers, we hope) as they discover so much more than what you'll see around the hotels.

Grenada: Key Facts

Location	12°N by 61°W
	90 miles (144 km) north of Trinidad
	2,200 miles (3546 km) southeast of New York
Size	133 square miles (344 square km)
	21 miles (34 km) long, 12 miles (19 km) wide
Highest point	Mt. St. Catherine. 2,756 feet (840 m)
Population	90,000
Language	English
Time	Atlantic Standard Time (1 hour ahead of EST, same as EDT)
Electricity	220 volts AC, 50 cycles, so transformers and adapters are necessary for U.S.-made appliances
Currency	The Eastern Caribbean dollar, EC$ (EC$2.68 = US$1)
Driving	On the LEFT; a valid U.S. or Canadian driver's license with a local permit ($12, issued by car-rental firms)
Area code	473
Documents	Valid passport (recommended), or proof of nationality with photo ID and an ongoing or return ticket
Departure tax	$20
Beer to drink	Carib
Rum to drink	Rivers
Music to hear	Dancehall
Tourism info	800-927-9554 or 212-687-9554
	www.grenadagrenadines.com

The Briefest History
(okay, maybe not so brief this time)

Grenada was first settled by Amerindians from South America. First came the Arawaks and then the Caribs. By the time Columbus sighted the island on his third voyage, in 1498, the Caribs were firmly entrenched, thus inhibiting European settlement until the 17th century, when the French defeated the Caribs in 1651. This is a famous battle: Rather than be conquered, the last band of Carib warriors tossed the women and children into the sea and then, in a suicide leap, plunged to their own deaths off Leapers' Hill (Le Morne de Sauteur) onto a rocky beach below.

After this conquest, Grenada, like so many other islands in the West Indies, became a pawn in the constant tug-of-war between the two chief rivals of the region, France and Britain. The island changed hands several times. Finally, in 1783, the Treaty of Versailles deeded the rights to Britain. Independence was granted almost 200 years later, when Grenada became an independent state in 1974, with Sir Eric Gairy at the helm.

Now, Sir Eric was a weird fellow (he believed in UFOs and said he communicated with them) and a demagogue. In 1979 Maurice Bishop, his chief rival both politically and ideologically, staged a coup d'état while Sir Eric was out of the country. Bishop was a Marxist who wanted closer relations with both Castro (his mentor) and the Soviet Union. Bishop ruled for four years, trying to institute socialist reforms in the country. It was when Bishop started making overtures to the U.S. that a rival faction in his New JEWEL (Joint Endeavor for Welfare, Education and Liberation) Movement, led by Bernard Coard, staged another coup d'état in 1983 and had Bishop and his close advisers arrested and executed.

The country reeled as news of this event spread throughout St. George's, and unrest was widespread and sudden. The U.S. and the leaders of several Caribbean island nations — led by Eugenia Charles of Dominica — viewed the alliance of Grenada and Cuba with great suspicion; both felt that Castro wanted to use Grenada as a military base (indeed, he was building an airport large enough to receive jet aircraft). So under the pretext of rescuing about 100 American students at the island's medical school, the U.S. invaded Grenada, expelled the Cubans (who put up armed resistance), and restored order. As a whole, Grenadians were very happy that the "troubles" were over, and appreciative of the American effort and especially of all the aid money that poured in afterward (there were a lot of new cars around a year after the intervention). Elections were held in 1984 to choose a new government, and since then things have been more peaceful on the Isle of Spice. The Point Salines Airport was completed and has subsequently provided Grenada a tourism advantage over neighboring islands with smaller, less modern facilities. The current prime minister and government are expanding the tourist infrastructure and are American-friendly. As for Castro, the Cuban leader made a goodwill visit to the country in 1998, with barely a peep of protest from Washington, D.C.

Getting There

The Point Salines International Airport is conveniently close to most tourist accommodations on the island (thanks, Fidel). Service to Grenada is available on **Air Jamaica** from New York, **American Eagle** from San Juan, on **US Airways** from Philadelphia; and on **BWIA** via Trinidad, connecting to flights out of Miami, New York, and Toronto. **Air Canada** flies in from Toronto; **British Airways** flies in from London. **LIAT** and **Caribbean Star** fly to Grenada from major destinations in the Eastern Caribbean, and **SVG Air** connects Grenada with Carriacou and Union islands.

Getting Around

There are plenty of taxis at the airport. A taxi to the Grand Anse or L'Anse aux Epines area will cost about $10, offically. Be prepared to be ambushed by cabbies when the Customs door slides open. Do haggle—the competition is fierce and you should win, although there are official rates posted. Don't let anyone grab your luggage until all financial matters are settled. There are also minivans or minibuses, which charge a dollar or so for trips between points in the southern part of the island. They ply the major roads from Grand Anse into St. George's and provide easy and fun transport. The vans blast dancehall music and bear names like "Ruff Xample," "Oo-la-la," "Log On," "Out-ah-Order" or "Tight Clothes." It's a great way to meet Grenadians.

There are plenty of rental cars available, too, although the roads outside the tourist area aren't always well paved and directions are poorly marked. **Avis/Spice Isle Rentals** (800-331-1084 or 473-440-

3936) and **Dollar** (800-421-6868 or 473-444-4786) have outposts here. Be sure to make your reservations well in advance to ensure the best rates.

The best way to see the island is with Dennis Henry of **Henry's Safari Tours** (473-444-5313, fax 473-444-4460; e-mail: safari@caribsurf.com). He'll show you the real Grenada (in a comfortable air-conditioned van) and take you on great hikes, too. One of his best is to Honeymoon Falls. It's a 3.5-hour hike that is no honeymoon (you must climb up a river for a way), but once you get there, ahhhhhhh. Dennis leads a number of other "safaris," too. Better still is Dennis himself. He has such a wealth of knowledge about his island and is a great, athletic, fun guy. Dennis also provisions sailboats, so if you're chartering out of Grenada, give him a call.

Focus on Grenada: Grenada Photo Safari

Grenada's physical beauty makes it a natural for the camera, but getting to your subject matter can prove difficult. There are several ways to photograph the island beyond the boundaries of your hotel. If you're comfortable with left-side driving, you can rent a car, and touring the southern part of Grenada (the most populated and touristed area) is easy. As you head north on either side of the island, however, you'll find that the roads are more narrow, winding, and sometimes rutted (but actual road conditions have been steadily improving for the last few years). Worse yet, you'll find few directional signs to point your way, although as you get lost you may stumble across some interesting sights. For those with a sense of adventure, there is the bus system — an experience in itself. This is a fine way to get to know Grenadians (to whom you'll be squeezed close), as you careen rapidly down the roads, dancehall music blaring.

If these options aren't what you had in mind, look no further than Dennis Henry. Henry's Safari Tours (473-444-5313) will take you for a six-hour tour, leaving at 9 a.m. from your hotel or guest house for $80 for one person, $35 each for three or more. Half-day tours are $60 for one or $25 each for three persons. Dennis, who goes by at least five names, will design a photo safari that will let you put the best of Grenada on film. You'll have frequent stops for photo ops, as well as a tasty lunch. The vehicle is a comfortable van with good visibility and height to let you take in as much as you can. Dennis is also an avid hiker and conducts mountain walking tours (see "Getting Around," above).

Camera Etiquette

Like some celebrities, many islanders get irritated when you snap a picture of them without their permission. To show courtesy and to avoid unpleasantness, ask before clicking the shutter. Sometimes a friendly gesture and a smile will do the trick. With group shots, use your judgment. A group of women washing clothes in a river may not mind a photo from a distance, whereas a group of Rastas toking on a spliff may feel their personal space has been invaded, and may end up taking the film—and maybe your camera—from you.

Photo Safari 1: St. George's

Photogenic St. George's is best seen on foot. The town, built on steep hills around a cozy harbor, has many stair accesses and roads too narrow for cars. It's easy to get to St. George's from your hotel, as you are never more than a few miles away by taxi, minibus, or thumb. Avoid this tour on a day when a cruise ship is calling on the island — you don't need couples in matching black socks cluttering your pictures.

Plan on doing the walk in the morning, because it gets too hot by lunchtime. Also, bright midday light bleaches the color and life out of your subjects. The hour or two before sunset warms up the color. The best place to start is at the Carenage. You'll find a Grentel office for overseas calls, a LIAT office to reconfirm your return flight, the tourist board to buy a good map, and even FedEx—all in a row. Across the street to the right, the mailboats *Alexia II* and *Adelaide B* and sailing schooner *Alexia III* depart on alternate days for Carriacou. These wooden boats with sails, mast, and so on may not inspire much confidence as a form of public transport or especially as pleasure craft, but it's possible to secure passage on one—a great experience. The more modern high-speed catamaran *Osprey Express* departs for Carriacou daily.

Moving along, you'll pass the former location of the Nutmeg—a good spot for lunch later on (or a rum punch now). Turn right on Young Street, and you'll pass the National Museum on the left. Admission is $2, and you can scour the island's history (up to and including the 1983 intervention) in 20 or 30 minutes.

When you're ready to move on, just past the museum on the opposite side of Young Street is the **Yellow Poui Art Gallery** (473-440-3001). This is a legitimate gallery, not a tourist joint, with the work of 85 artists from around the world on display, including a number of Grenadian and West Indian painters. Prices are not too high, and it's worth a look. Owner Jim Rudin is very knowledgeable and will show you the latest from Caliste (a primitive painter from Carriacou who is much in favor). Yellow Poui is located just upstairs from Art Fabrik, a store that sells attractive batik pieces.

At Church Street, take a right and follow it all the way past several good examples of both English- and French-influenced island architecture—including the Anglican church and the cathedral—that dominates the top of the hill. Then cruise down Market Hill to Market Square, where tables are set up and anyone can come in and sell their wares. This very picturesque area can be mobbed on cruise ship days, but it's a good place to strike up a conversation, especially in one of the surrounding rum shops.

You're on the homestretch now. Take a left on Church Street, right on Simmons, and down the steps to Scott Street and the Carenage. That should put you right at the Nutmeg for lunch (and a much-needed rum punch).

Photo Safari 2: Northern Grenada

For this expedition, you need a guide. The roads aren't marked and are often in bad shape—your AAA card won't work here. The guide will show you places you could never find on your own. Alternatively, have a good navigator with a copy of a recent map to help steer your way.

This is an all-day affair. From St. George's, head up the western road. As soon as you leave the capital you'll be on your way into the real Grenada. Some of the photographic highlights you should encounter are described below.

Laundry

Never did laundry look so photogenic. Along the west coast you will often encounter women doing laundry in the rivers. The light is muted from the green canopy, and the subjects are almost always interesting from any angle.

Concord Falls

A one-lane road snakes up the hill past countless nutmeg trees to the falls. Get out of the car and walk up to the Fontainebleu Falls (which takes about 30 minutes) — it's much prettier. There are lush greens with peaked hills as background.

Rum shops

One thing becomes clear as you drive around Grenada (and most other West Indian islands): It seems as though every other house has a liquor license. These shops sell sundries as well as drinks, so you can have a rum punch while looking at the eggs and crackers. Now that's progress.

Douglaston Estate

This is a spice-processing station near Concord. Outside, there are several drying racks on rollers. Should it start to rain, they are swiftly pushed into the workhouse, to be rolled out when the sun shines again. Inside, women separate the mace from the nutmeg seed as well as prepare cocoa and coffee beans, cinnamon, and bay leaves. The faces of the workers alone are worth the trip.

Gouyave

Pronounced "guave," this is Grenada's nutmeg-processing station (the next stop after Douglaston). Gouyave is notorious for its loony citizens, who seem to burn the midnight oil more here than anywhere else on the island. There is also a sizable fishing community, whose odd hours may add to the general wackiness. Every Sunday evening, there is a festive jump-up in the street with dancehall music.

Women with things balanced on their heads

You won't see this on the streets of New York. These women have strong necks. It's astonishing what they can balance. Bonus points if you can snap a woman carrying a case of Coke or Carib on her head.

Prospect

If the bridge is out, or just for the fun of it, take the road through this area. It's real Grenadian backcountry, with fine examples of rural dwellings.

Sauteurs

After Prospect, the road will suddenly end on a beach with a commanding view of Sauteurs and its cathedral on top of Leapers' Hill (Le Morne de Sauteur). The town itself is quaint and worth a brief tour with camera in hand. The drive up to the cathedral will bring you to Leapers' Hill, where the last re-maining Carib Indians leaped to their deaths rather than be captured by their French pursuers. At the church, a busy workshop of the Young Grenadians United Crafts Workers Association produces candles and batik that can be bought on the spot. These are teenagers trying to make a cooperative succeed—a worthy effort. In front of the workshop is an old cemetery, and beyond an excellent view of Carriacou.

Morne Fendue

Home of the Morne Fendue Plantation Great House, where you should plan on having lunch. The charming Great House was built of gray stone and wrought iron in 1908. There are several varieties of brilliant flowering shrubs and the biggest red poinsettias we've ever seen.

Rive Antoine

Several miles outside Morne Fendue, the road will emerge from the hinterland onto a windswept, palm-studded beach called Bathaway that curves around to some gigantic cliffs to the north. This is a good place to sit, cool off, and enjoy the view. If you swim, beware of the undertow (there's a natural "swimming hole" formed in the coral).

Right up the road from the beach is the Rive Antoine rum distillery. After driving through fields of sugarcane—many charred from the annual harvest burning—you'll arrive at some old stone buildings and the distillery's huge waterwheel. This is one of the few remaining distilleries that looks and operates the way it did more than 150 years ago.

There are four stages in the Rive Antoine distilling process. The first is the crushing station, where a big waterwheel squishes the juice from the cane stalks, then sluices the liquid into the next stage—the boiling room. In this cavernous barn, five tanks bubble the juice at different temperatures while birds and bats fly in and out around the rafters, adding their "seasoning" to the batch. It is then sluiced off again to the fermenting and storage room. After aging, it goes to the still to be boiled to its clear white state. Unfortunately, you can't sample it here due to strict Grenada laws regarding liquor taxes. Only the Customs man has the key. However, it's sold in just about any rum shop by the glass and in a few liquor stores in St. George's, under the Rivers label.

Pearl's Airport

This rock-strewn strip with cattle grazing on the side used to be the international airport. See if you can spot the burned-out remains of an Aeroflot and a Cubana Airways airplane. A reminder of what used to be.

Grenville

A fishing and boat-building center with good waterfront and boat photo potential. Get out of the car and check it out. Then head south through the basket-weaving district. It seems as if everyone is weaving. Stop and ask about the craft, perhaps buy something, and ask to take a picture.

Grand Etang National Park

It's been a long, hot day, but you're almost home. Don't worry, you won't be hiking (save that for another day), just driving through Grenada's rain forest. There will be points along the snaking road with nice vistas of both the forest vegetation and St. George's in the distance.

Where to Stay

Almost all of Grenada's accommodations are found on the southwestern corner of the island, from St. George's to the tip of L'Anse aux Epines. Many of the hotels are on or within walking distance of Grenada's most popular beach, Grand Anse. Some good news: Grenada has a wide variety of rooms in the moderate to low-budget range, as well as several nice luxury properties. A new resort and golf complex to be located at Ladera, near the northern tip of the island, is being developed.

⊛ **Grenada Grand Beach Resort**, P.O. Box 441, Grand Anse Beach, Grenada, W.I. ℂ 473-444-4371, ✆ 473-444-4800, 🖳 www.grandbeach.net, paradise@grandbeach.net

🛄 **Very Pricey** ⑪ **EP** ⒸⒸ

If you want a big, comfortable, no-surprises resort, this is a good choice. Located in the middle of Grand Anse Beach— the best spot on the best beach in Grenada—this hotel delivers ample tropical setting, and as big resorts go, it's not bad-looking, particularly since the addition of a huge freeform swimming pool with waterfalls and greenery touches. The 185 original rooms, situated in two-story wings, are a decent size and attractive, with air conditioning, balcony or veranda, phone, satellite TV, and room service. An expansion of the resort opened in 2002 and added 60 new rooms in an adjacent four-story building overlooking the beach—while we wish they had done something less lofty, the view is nice and these rooms are in better condition (until a planned upgrade perks up the older units). There are two lighted tennis courts, all water sports, and an activities desk, plus two restaurants and three bars. The clientele here tends to be younger than at some of the neighboring resorts, except when a convention rolls into town and takes over the resort's copious meeting facilities.

Spice Island Beach Resort, Grand Anse Beach, P.O. Box 6, St. George's, Grenada, W.I. ℂ Stateside: 800-742-4276, Local: 473-444-4258, ✆ 473-444-4807, 🖳 www.spicebeach-resort.com, spiceisl@caribsurf.com

🛍 **Beyond Belief** ⑪ **All-inclusive** (motorized watersports and diving extra) Ⓒ

Situated on a quarter-mile stretch of beautiful Grande Anse Beach and next door to the infamous St. George's School of Medicine (remember those poor, unfortunate beachside med students who just had to be saved from anarchy and sunburn in Ronald Reagan's B-movieish Invasion of Grenada), this resort offers a variety of suites with private pools, whirlpools, saunas, and beachfront views. It also boasts Spice Island Divers, a complete dive and water-sports facility. All rooms have minibars, hair dryers, air conditioning, ceiling fans, radios, telephones, safes, coffee machines, beach towels, chaise longues, and a patio or balcony. There are pool suites that have a semiprivate pool (somewhat larger than a plunge pool) and a terrace for sunning—sweet! If you stay in one of the beach suites, your chaise lounge will be brought out to the beach for you each morning. The resort recently completed a $5.5 million renovation that upgraded some of the rooms, rebuilt the bar and dining areas, and added a pleasing freeform pool.

Breakfast and dinner are served in the open-air beachfront restaurant (you might have to do a Tippi Hedren at breakfast to keep the birds from stealing your food). Lunch is served in the adjacent bar restaurant. The food is standard continental fare along with a nice touch of local dishes, including Grenadian Night (Wednesdays), when a buffet of wonderful local foods and live entertainment are provided. The renovation also added a small fitness center and health spa. The clientele tends to be a bit older (like, over 50), although the management has introduced a new honeymoon package to attract a younger crowd. There's even a wedding package complete with cake, photos, and a best man or maid of honor. How about offering a bride or groom, too?

Blue Horizons Cottage Hotel, P.O. Box 41, St. George's, Grenada, W.I. ⒸStateside: 800-742-4276, Local: 473-444-4316, ✆ 473-444-2815, 🖳 blue@caribsurf.com

🛍 **Pricey** 🍴 **EP** Ⓒ🄲

Nestled within six acres of tropical gardens with a private aviary featuring 21 species of tropical birds, Blue Horizon is a good value. There are 32 cottage-style rooms (six Superior studio units and 26 Deluxe suites). All rooms have air conditioning, ceiling fan, color television, hair dryer, telephone, clock radio, and kitchenette featuring a refrigerator, stove, and ample counter space. You are just a short walk from Grande Anse Beach and can partake in various beach activities offered at their sister property, Spice Island Beach Resort (an added bonus). The hotel has a renowned restaurant, La Belle Créole, which features nouvelle West Indian cuisine.

The Flamboyant Hotel, P.O. Box 214, St. George's, Grenada, W.I. ⒸStateside: 800-223-9815, Local: 473-444-4247, ✆ 473-444-1234, 🖳 www.flamboyant.com, flambo@caribsurf.com

🛍 **Not So Cheap** 🍴 Ⓒ🄲

The name alone is reason to stay here (it's actually the name of a brilliant flowering tree found in these parts). The Flamboyant is a complex of 61 cottages and apartments on a hill, with a terrific view of Grand Anse and St. George's in the distance. They are functional in design and come with one or two bedrooms, kitchenette, living and dining room, and front porch from which to enjoy the view. The grounds are nicely landscaped, and a footpath offers a five-minute walk down to the beach. There's a restaurant, bar and pool, and a super-market about a mile down the road.

⊛ **Laluna Resort,** Morne Rouge, P.O. Box 1500, St. George's, Grenada, W.I. ℂ Stateside: 866-452-5862, Local: 473-439-0001, ✎ 473-439-0600, 🖳 www.laluna.com, info@laluna.com

💲 **Ridiculous** 🍴 **EP** (CC)

This is Grenada's newest accommodation, and if it looks like it just stepped out of some swanky fashion magazine, it's not by accident. The owner and developer is an Italian fashion maven, Bernardo Bertucci (with backing from Benetton and Zegna), and it seems he is aiming for the Grenadian equivalent of world beat-style accommodations. Situated in a heretofore undeveloped cove just south of Grand Anse, Laluna is designed with a Moorish sensibility, with lots of richly painted cement — sienna, violet, and amber hues dominate. Each of the 16 cottages is identical (only one is next to the sand), with king-size beds facing the view and adorned with mosquito nets. Straw mats, lots of pillows, and very attractive Indonesian furniture like day beds fill the space. Amenities include CD player, TV with VCR, minibar, tea and coffee maker, and air conditioning. Bathrooms have an outdoor shower, and on the terrace is your own plunge pool. The main area has a thatch-roof restaurant (again, with lots of sexy Indonesian accents), and there is a large common-area pool. The beach is small but wonderful and uncrowded. Although there's a lot of high style, there's not much attitude — the place sells laid back.

Our only complaint is that there's a good deal of surface here, and not enough foundation — we mean this both literally and figuratively. The restaurant — which blends Italian, Caribbean, and Asian elements in its menu, is quite expensive, and although we didn't dine here, we heard both positive and negative comments. Still, for the moment, this is the island's exclusive encounter with chic fashions found in places like St. Barts.

Calabash, P.O. Box 382, L'Anse aux Epines, St. George's, Grenada, W.I. ✆ Stateside: 800-528-5835, Local: 473-444-4334, 🖂 473-444-5050, 🖳 www.calabashhotel.com, calabash@caribsurf.com

💲 **Beyond Belief** for standard rooms and **Stratospheric** for the pool suites 🍴 **BP** 🆑

Calabash is perhaps Grenada's most deluxe digs. The two-story cottages house 30 spacious suites, decorated with tropical prints and white tile floors — eight of which have a totally private plunge pool in back. Full breakfast is included in the rates, prepared and served by a maid in your room each morning. Located on eight acres on tranquil L'Anse aux Epines Beach, the atmosphere here is casual and the grounds and beach are quite pleasant. There's a pool, a lighted tennis court, an aromatherapy room and a small gym, and afternoon tea is served daily. The restaurant is one of the best on the island, with a new wine cellar. The staff is attentive and upbeat; however, they're not much up on the "real" Grenada — another reason to ring Dennis Henry for island explorations.

L'anse aux Epines Cottages, P.O. Box 187, St. George's, Grenada, W.I. ✆ 473-444-4565, 🖂 473-444-2802, 🖳 www.laecottages.com, cottages@caribsurf.com

💲 **Not So Cheap** 🍴 **EP** 🆑

With beautiful coconut palm–studded grounds and a nice beach out front with lots of shade (it shares the beach with Calabash), this property features attractive stone and wrought-iron cottages with green tin roofs. All cottages are screened and have fully equipped kitchens, ceiling fans, air-conditioned bedrooms, and TV. Also included is full maid service — she'll clean, cook, and do light laundry, a definite plus. Don't stay in the apartments, though; they look like prisons.

Coral Cove Cottages and Apartments, L'Anse aux Epines, P.O. Box 487, St. George's, Grenada, W.I. ✆ 473-444-4422,

✆ 473-444-4718, 🖳 www.coralcovecottages.com,
coralcv@caribsurf.com

💰 **Not So Cheap** ⑪ **EP** ⒸⒸ

This is a nice little place on the water, located in a quiet residential area punctuated by foreign embassies. Guests have a choice of 11 simple but comfortable cottages or apartments, all with fully equipped kitchens, lanais, maid service, and ceiling fans. There are one- and two-bedroom units available, making this a great family option. The beach is not much, but it is private and the snorkeling is good, and there is a tennis court and pool for your leisure.

Siesta Hotel, P.O. Box 27, Grand Anse, Grenada, W.I. ✆ Stateside: 800-742-4276, Local: 473-444-4645, ✆ 473-444-4647, 🖳 www.siestahotel.com, siesta@caribsurf.com

💰 **Cheap** ⑪ **EP** ⒸⒸ

Ideally located about 200 yards from the beach at Grand Anse, this hotel is a well-run find that offers 37 simply furnished but attractive and clean air-conditioned rooms, a pool, and a restaurant (no alcohol). Standard rooms are just that, or you can get a studio suite.

Wave Crest Holiday Apartments, P.O. Box 278, St. George's, Grenada, W.I. ✆ 473-444-4116, ✆ same as phone, 🖳 www.grenadawavecrest.com, wavecrest@caribsurf.com

💰 **Cheap** ⑪ **EP** ⒸⒸ

Situated on a residential hillside behind Grand Anse, Wave Crest is a great buy, with attentive managers. The 18 units have air conditioning, verandas, and basic kitchens. Furnishings are a little tired but adequate for anyone on a no-frills vacation. The beach is a 10-minute walk, and grocery stores and restaurants are nearby; note that there's a fair amount of road traffic during the day.

⊛ **La Sagesse Nature Centre**, P.O. Box 44, St. David's, Grenada, W.I. ℂ 473-444-6458, ⌾ 473-444-6458, ▭ www.lasagesse.com, lsnature@caribsurf.com

💼 **Not So Cheap** ⓦ **EP** ⒸⒸ

If you're looking for a quiet place to stay that's off the beaten path, La Sagesse may be for you. Located well away from the commotion of Grand Anse, La Sagesse is an informal nine-room country house next to a tranquil Atlantic-facing beach. The rebuilt Manor House contains five of the rooms, just 30 feet from the sand; one has air conditioning. There's a two-room cottage, and a new building (completed in 2002 in the location of the old restaurant) has five new rooms, all facing the sea. There's a solid restaurant serving breakfast, lunch, and dinner, along with decent swimming, miles of nature trails, and 77 acres of banana fields and cow pastures to contemplate.

Bel Air Plantation, St. David's, Grenada, W.I. ℂ 473-444-6305, ⌾ 473-444-6316, ▭ www.belairplantation.com, belair@caribsurf.com

💼 **Very Pricey** ⓦ **EP** ⒸⒸ

Overlooking St. David's Harbour, this intimate new resort opened in early 2003 on the site of Grenada's first European settlement, where the French landed in 1650. American developer Susan Fisher chose the lush, 18-acre, Atlantic-facing peninsula—located just south of La Sagesse—as a refuge from busy beachfront resorts and named it after her mother's one-time plantation in Guyana. The 11 (of 24 planned) cottages and villas are fringed in gingerbread and vibrant colors, equipped with kitchens, original island art, and bathrooms replete with Jacuzzi tubs and tiles from Italy and Portugal. Each unit is positioned to maximize both privacy and panorama of the bay from a veranda. A woodworking shop produces much of Bel Air's handcrafted furniture. Pathways are made from nutmeg shells (the island exports a third of the world's supply of the spice), and considerable attention has been paid to landscaping—20 different varieties of hibiscus for starters, and the nursery grows sugar apples, Surinam cherries, and herbs and vegetables for the restaurant. Activities include a swimming pool, day sails, and snorkeling (when the water is calm) around the wreck of the one-time cargo ship Orinocco, which foundered off the tip of the peninsula in 1900.

Where to Eat

There is not a huge selection of great restaurants, but there are a few good places.

$$$$ ⊛ **Aquarium**, Pink Gin Beach, 473-444-1410
This is one of our favorite hangouts in the Caribbean. A driveway heads down a gully to a parking lot and path, leading into a grottolike setting trimmed by a waterfall on one side and a gorgeous beach on the other. Lunch is the perfect time to experience it all, when you can arrange for a kayak or snorkeling spin before your meal. Food is satisfying and dependable, if a bit expensive, but the ambiance, replete with great music, is perfect.

$$$ **The Boatyard**, Spice Island Marina, L'Anse aux Epines, 473-444-4662
The only reason we mention this haunt of the yachty set is that when we came here the first time, Senator Ted Kennedy was sitting at the next table. We found the grilled meats dreadful, but liquid dinners are the vogue among boaters, anyway. Live steel band on Fridays until late at night.

$$$ **Coconut Beach**, Grand Anse, 473-444-4644
Located on the beach in a wonderful old funky house, this establishment features good Creole cuisine in a romantic yet casual setting. Reservations are suggested. Closed Tuesday.

$$$$ **La Belle Creole,** Blue Horizon Cottage Hotel, Grand Anse, 473-444-4316
Thought by some to be the best restaurant on Grenada, La Belle Creole features heavy, rich West Indian food (local dishes with a Continental flourish). We think it's expensive for what you get, and service is a bit stuffy. Reservations are required.

$$$$$ **Laluna,** Morne Rouge, 473-439-0001
Intimate, romantic, pricey. If you've got a few extra bucks, it might be worth a splurge. Italian meets island with Asian accents and a great wine list.

$$ ⊛**La Sagesse,** La Sagesse Nature Centre, 473-444-6458
The restaurant at this hideaway tenders delicious seafood and sandwiches at modest prices. La Sagesse offers a smart day-trip package: round-trip transportation from any island hotel, a guided nature walk, and lunch (or dinner), all for $28 per person.

$$ **Morne Fendue Plantation Great House,** St. Patrick's Parish, 473-442-9330
A classic old plantation house, Morne Fendue is located in the heart of Grenada's northern hills. The house is made of gray stone with wrought-iron grillwork and huge poinsettias in the circular driveway. When you arrive for lunch, you are greeted and sent (ordered) to the washroom to freshen up. The cuisine is traditional West Indian: callaloo soup, ox tail and tongue, seasoned rice, chicken, christophene, and papaya custard and cream are typical fare. Morne Fendue was the home of Betty Mascol for most of the 20th century, but she passed away in 1998. The home was purchased by Jean Thompson, who carries on the tradition of this time-honored establishment. Mrs. Mascol's pepper pot lives on! Lunch is about $15. No credit cards.

$$ **The Nutmeg,** on the Carenage, St. George's, 473-440-2539
The rum punch is fantastic, which may be the best reason to go here. The food is decent, the place clean, and the second

floor offers commendable views of the harbor. Their fish specials and lambi (conch) are recommended, and be sure to
check out the nutmeg ice cream. A great spot for breakfast
and lunch in town.

Going Out

There are some fun things to do here at night. **The Boatyard** at
L'Anse aux Epines Beach in the Marina has a popular Friday and Saturday night party with a steel band and a local DJ. ✪ **Fantazia 2001
Disco**, at the Gem Apartments on Morne Rouge Beach (473-444-1189),
is the island's hot dance palace and is very popular with locals (no
shorts). Wednesday is '70s music.

Don't Miss

Henry's Safari Tours

You won't be disappointed.

Foodland

If you have an efficiency, this is a great supermarket located
in the Grand Anse Shopping Center.

Carriacou

Grenada's sister island (see the Carriacou chapter).

Dive Grenada

The island's oldest dive shop, located on Grand Anse. It does
trips to the wreck of the *Bianca C*, the largest shipwreck in the
Caribbean (a 584-foot Italian cruise ship that went down in
1961 after a boiler explosion), and it is suitable for advanced
divers. Easier sites, too, as well as daily snorkel excursions for
$20. Call 473-444-1092 or go to www.divegrenada.com.

Grand Etang

An extinct volcanic crater nestled in the mountains above St.
George's. On a clear day, this is a splendid sight, and a lovely
trail circuits the lake. An eclectic mix of wildlife hangs out
here, including mona monkeys, freshwater crayfish, and a variety of birds.

⊛The Saturday Marketplace in St. George's

This weekly event is a wonderful venue to glimpse a classic of West Indian life, the open-air market. It's colorful, it's lively, it's tasty, and it's real. It's also a great place to shop (and bargain) for souvenirs. Go early, before the heat of the day saps your energy.

INDEX

WRITE TO RUM & REGGAE

Dear Rum & Reggae Caribbean Readers,

We really do appreciate and value your comments, suggestions, or information about anything new or exciting in the Caribbean. We'd love to hear about your experiences, good and bad, while you were in the tropics. Your feedback will help us to shape the next edition. So please let us hear from you.

Visit our Web site at: www.rumreggae.com,
e-mail us at yahmon@rumreggae.com, or write to:

> Mr. Yah Mon
> Rum & Reggae Guidebooks
> P.O. Box 130153
> Boston, MA 02113

> Sincerely,
>
> *Jonathan Runge*

P.S We often mention cocktails, drinking, and other things in this book. We certainly do not mean to upset any nondrinkers or those in Recovery. Please don't take offense—rum and its relatives are not a requirement for a successful vacation in the Caribbean.

ABOUT THE AUTHOR

JONATHAN RUNGE is the author of thirteen travel books: *Rum & Reggae's Grenadines, Including St. Vincent and Grenada* (2003), *Rum & Reggae's Virgin Islands* (2003), *Rum & Reggae's Caribbean* (2002), *Rum & Reggae's Jamaica* (2002), *Rum & Reggae's Puerto Rico* (2002), *Rum & Reggae's Dominican Republic* (2002), *Rum & Reggae's Cuba* (2002), *Rum & Reggae's Hawai'i* (2001), *Rum & Reggae's Caribbean 2000* (2000), *Rum & Reggae: The Insider's Guide to the Caribbean* (Villard Books, 1993); *Hot on Hawai'i: The Definitive Guide to the Aloha State* (St. Martin's Press, 1989); *Rum & Reggae: What's Hot and What's Not in the Caribbean* (St. Martin's Press, 1988); and *Ski Party!: The Skier's Guide to the Good Life*, co-authored with Steve Deschenes (St. Martin's Press, 1985). Jonathan has also written for *Men's Journal, Outside, National Geographic Traveler, Out, Skiing, Boston*, and other magazines. He is also the publisher and principal owner of Rum & Reggae Guidebooks, Inc., based in Massachusetts. Books to be published in 2003 from Jonathan Runge and Rum & Reggae Guidebooks include: *Rum & Reggae's Brasil* and *Rum & Reggae's French Caribbean*.

RUM & REGGAE'S
TOURISTO SCALE

1. What century is this?

2. Tiny or no airport, or political upheaval keeps tourists away.

3. A nice, unspoiled yet civilized place.

4. Still unspoiled, but getting popular.

5. A popular place, but still not too developed.

6. Busy and booming; this was very quiet not long ago.

7. Well-developed tourism and lots of tourists;
fast-food outlets conspicuous.

8. Highly developed and tons of tourists.

9. Mega-tourists and tour groups;
fast-food outlets outnumber restaurants.

10. Swarms of tourists and total development.
Run for cover!